MW00460500

LANGUAGES OF THE NIGHT

BARRY MCCREA

Languages of the Night

Minor Languages and the Literary Imagination

in Twentieth-Century Ireland and Europe

Yale UNIVERSITY PRESS

NEW HAVEN AND LONDON

Yale University Press books may be purchased in quantity
for educational, business, or promotional use. For information, please e-mail sales.press@yale.edu (U.S. office) or
sales@yaleup.co.uk (U.K. office).

Set in Janson Oldstyle and Futura Bold types by Newgen North America.
Printed in the United States of America.

Library of Congress Cataloging-in-Publication Data
McCrea, Barry, 1974–
Languages of the night : minor languages and the literary imagination in
twentieth-century Ireland and Europe / Barry McCrea.
pages   cm
Includes bibliographical references and index.
ISBN 978-0-300-18515-7 (hardback)
1. Linguistic minorities—Europe—Cross-cultural studies.   2. Experimental
poetry—20th century—History and criticism—Great Britain.   3. Experimental
poetry—20th century—History and criticism—Europe.   I. Title.
P120.L34M337 2015
401'.9—dc23
2014028310

A catalogue record for this book is available from the British Library.

This paper meets the requirements of ANSI/NISO Z39.48-1992
(Permanence of Paper).
10 9 8 7 6 5 4 3 2 1

For
Ronan McCrea
and
Caitríona Ní Dhúill

Parlavo a un popolo di morti. Morto alloro rifiuto e chiedo oblio.
—Umberto Saba, "Epigrafe"

I spoke to a people who were dead. Dead, I
spurn the laurel and ask oblivion.
(Translation by George Hochfield and Leonard Nathan
in *Songbook: The Selected Poems of Umberto Saba*)

Is í an bán-martra do dhuine, an tan scaras,
as son Dé, re gach rud a charas.

This is white martyrdom to a person: to
renounce everything one loves for God.
—Early Irish Sermon

CONTENTS

The emergence of vernacular literature—how, when, and why a spoken tongue is adopted for written purposes—is a well known and much studied process. This book is concerned with the opposite phenomenon: the unique possibilities offered to the literary imagination by languages as they fall out of use as spoken mediums of daily life.

Throughout much of Europe at the beginning of the twentieth century, to travel through the countryside was to hear the language spoken around you change with the landscape, often every few miles. Whether it was a case of historically separate languages, such as Breton, Gaelic, and Basque, in all their local varieties, or continuums of dialects that varied between one village and the next, such as Francoprovençal or Low German, most people in rural Europe spoke a language or a dialect that was bound not only to a region but often to a specific valley or village. In large parts of the Continent, every patch of territory and every small community had its own unique speech, a form of language with which it was possible for an identifiable group to have a wholly intimate relationship. Between roughly 1850 and 1950, however, populations all over western Europe began to abandon these idioms that had dominated the speech of country people for centuries, and switched to using standard, transregional metropolitan languages, such as English, French, High German, or Italian—languages that had in some cases previously been used only for written or formal purposes—as the spoken language of local and family life.

Precisely as this dramatic transformation was taking place in the linguistic life of rural Europe, in the cities modernist writers were searching for new forms of literary language for poetry and for prose. This book is about the links between these two phenomena: the sudden linguistic homogenization of the European countryside and the rise of modernist impulses among writers in the European cities, writers who were driven by a feeling that language had become enervated and inauthentic, and who were animated by the desire to find or invent new linguistic forms for literary expression. *Languages of the Night* argues that for many writers the sense that language had become tired and alienated, and the hope that it might somehow be invigorated with new life, found a concrete correspondence in the vanishing vernaculars of the European peasant world. *Languages of the Night* is thus in some ways a challenge to the assumption that modernism is a literary mode of the city, showing how the dead, dying, or forgotten languages of the countryside had significant literary afterlives that were fundamental, in their own way, to the development of European modernism. As they fell out of use as the speech of everyday life, these declining vernaculars became unlikely repositories for a host of modernist dreams, expectations, and disappointments about what language could or should do.

Recent studies in modernist literature have sought to decenter Europe and "Eurochronology" as a whole from our models of literary history.[1] These are admirable and indeed necessary efforts, but they can also run the risk of lumping all of Europe into a single imaginary "metropole" or "center" and reducing it to a handful of major languages.[2] The inadvertent result is to further erase those dissonant and marginal forms of literary expression within Europe that spoke from places and lifeworlds far removed from metropolitan centers: writers, dialects, or languages whose voices are weirder and weaker, whose contributions to modernist literature and thought are hard to detect until one goes looking for them. This is not simply a case of uneven development, of minor languages somehow discovering metropolitan literary techniques, still less a project of spotlighting lesser-known nations, regions, or communities with their "own" literary traditions.[3] Instead, this book is about how the disappearance of minor languages and dialects from everyday life, or the apparent threat of their disappearance, lent them an imaginative power for modernist literature. In some cases, writers deliberately chose a disappearing dialect or minor language over their own major mother tongue, in others, the encounter with minor languages and dialects deeply affected the work of writers in a major language.

For the purposes of this book, the term "minor language" refers to a specific linguistic history rather than to raw numbers of speakers or to any philological definition. The political concept of a linguistic minority is not relevant here. Nor are we concerned with the linguistic consequences of migration (such as the Albanian speakers of southern Italy) or of shifting political borders (such as German speakers in South Tyrol). Languages which had relatively few speakers but which remained the ordinary spoken language of their historic population, such as Maltese and Faroese, are equally not at issue. The book instead explores the effects of those languages and dialects that, having been spoken by their communities for many centuries, began to fall out of everyday spoken use in the course of the nineteenth and twentieth centuries, abandoned by large numbers of their own speakers in favor of powerful national or international languages, such as English, French, and Italian. In some cases (such as northern French "patois" or Italian dialects) these minor languages are closely related to the standard, in others (such as Irish) we are dealing with highly distinct languages barely related to the language that supplanted them. These have very different histories (most notably, Irish had a long high literary life, whereas some Romance dialects were rarely even written down). The intention is not to elide these differences, but for the purposes of this book, the old and vexed distinction between language and dialect is not relevant. Our concern is with a change in the spoken medium of everyday life, whether it be a language, a dialect, or something contested or in between.

In most cases we are not dealing with languages and dialects that became extinct as vernaculars (though many of the patois of the Île-de-France that are the subject of the last chapter are no longer spoken as mother tongues). Rather, as they became rarer, or threatened to become so, these languages and dialects went on to have second, post-vernacular lives as literary mediums or sites of projection for writers for whom they were not a native language. The subject of this book is these later existences, the ways in which, despite all the odds, these languages persisted even into our hyper-globalized, late capitalist age, and how they shaped metropolitan literary culture.

The strange second wind that some of these minor languages experienced contributed to modernism in two distinct but related ways: in prose, minor languages exerted a fundamental if not always immediately visible influence on the work of modernist novelists in major languages who witnessed—whether at first or second hand—their decline as spoken vernaculars; in poetry, they were harnessed as experimental literary vehicles by poets who were native speakers of major languages but who thought they perceived in minor languages or dialects a purer alternative to what they saw as their own compromised or degraded major mother tongues. *Languages of the Night* links this second, relatively obscure strain of late modernist writing, whereby poets appropriated dwindling rural vernaculars as private languages of poetry, with the first, the formal and linguistic innovations of the high modernism. The principal examples of novelists in the book are Joyce and Proust (though the fate of minor languages continued to exercise an influence on later European novelists such as Giorgio Bassani and W. G. Sebald), and the chief (but not sole) examples of nonnative minor-language writing are the poems in Irish by the Cork poet Seán Ó Ríordáin and the early dialect poetry of Pier Paolo Pasolini. Minor-language poetry by nonnative speakers is often assumed to be part of revivalist activities with purely local or nationalist concerns. This book argues, however, that this unusual poetic tradition is not a neo-Romanticist or primitivist cult of authenticity but rather a form of modernist expressionism.

Chapter 1 gives an account of how, as its sociolinguistic circumstances changed over the twentieth century, the Irish language became the object of intense psychological and symbolic investments. The chapter opens with an analysis of how the disappearance of the Irish language as a mass vernacular engaged the imagination of James Joyce in ways that have little to do with political issues such as colonialism or national independence. It goes on to trace the changing ways in which Irish has been the focus of a variety of utopian longings beyond questions of nationalism or cultural revival. Chapter 2 explores the phenomenon of what I call literary white martyrdom in the early lyric poetry of Pier Paolo Pasolini. In Italy, unlike Ireland, there is a long tradition of thinking about language choice as a purely literary question, and specifically of the employment of minor speech varieties (dialect) as a literary *technique* or device rather than as an emblem of regional loyalty or political statement. Pasolini consciously exploited the rural dialects of Friuli, of which he was not a native speaker, as a means to invent a private, poetic language of his own and in order, paradoxically, to express the dislocations of modernity, and of queerness in particular. Chapter 3 uses the comparative framework offered by Pasolini's dialect poetry to explore the question of language choice in the poetry of Seán Ó Ríordáin, generally credited with the founding of a modernist literature in the Irish language. Ó Ríordáin bitterly lamented the fact that Irish was not his native language, yet he never wrote poetry in English. The chapter uses the comparison with Pasolini and Italian dialect writing to put the question of his language choice at the center of the meaning of Ó Ríordáin's work, suggesting that his use of Irish can be understood not as a patriotic or revivalist decision but as a form of expressionism. Chapter 4 returns to the era of high modernism to show how the disappearing rustic dialects of the Île-de-France haunt the modernist ideas of Marcel Proust. The last traces of the local patois, the mother tongue of the narrator's housekeeper, Françoise, are woven throughout *À la Recherche du temps perdu* (*In Search of Lost Time*) as privileged portals of access to an imaginary reality outside of and impervious to time.

Note: Except where otherwise stated, all translations are my own.

ACKNOWLEDGMENTS

This book has benefited from the generosity and insight of many colleagues and friends. It was begun during a year-long associate professor leave from Yale University, without which it could never have been written. It was also supported by the Yale Fund for Lesbian and Gay Studies, the Yale Heyman Prize for Outstanding Scholarly Publication in the Humanities, the Notre Dame Institute for Scholarship in the Liberal Arts, and the Keough-Naughton Institute for Irish Studies.

At Yale University Press, I acknowledge the work and help of Jeffrey Schier, Erica Hanson, and Otto Bohlmann.

My thanks to John Conlan for his work on the index.

I am grateful to An Cló IarChonnacht for permission to reprint Ó Ríordáin's poetry as well as excerpts from his letters and diaries.

A number of people read the manuscript, some at multiple stages, and, while all errors and infelicities remain my own, I owe them a huge debt of gratitude. Without Alison MacKeen, the book would never have seen the light of day. Maria DiBattista, wise and generous ally in so many things, first encouraged me to turn these ideas into a book. David Quint, Katie Trumpener, Matteo Residori, and Alexander Beecroft were all immensely helpful both in details of the manuscript and in thinking through its overall theoretical conception. Éric Trudel was of crucial help in many ways, most of all in his careful reading of the Proust chapter. Eric Hayot offered a last-minute and penetrating critique of style and other matters in the Introduction. Thanks for help with bibliographic and other details in the manuscript are due to Francesca Geymonat, Gréagóir Ó Dúill, Caitríona Ó Torna, and Jill Wharton. I am grateful also to a number of anonymous readers: those who reported on the manuscript for Yale University Press and those who reviewed my Yale tenure file.

The book was begun at one institution and finished at another, and it has benefited from the kindness and professionalism of colleagues at both. At Yale, in addition to the former colleagues mentioned above, I would like to record my gratitude to Dudley Andrew and Mary Jane Stevens. The origins of this book were in a talk I gave as a visiting speaker to the Ph.D. in Literature program at Notre Dame; this invitation had many consequences, apart from the book itself, and I am grateful to Tobias Boes for it. Among my new colleagues at Notre Dame I would like to thank Valerie Sayers, Chris Fox, Kate Marshall, Mary O'Callaghan, Beth Bland, Margaret Lloyd, Lynn McCormack, Karmen Duke, John McGreevy, Lisa Caulfield, and Kevin Whelan. The staff at Notre Dame's centers in Rome and Dublin are also due thanks, as are two former Domers, Maud Ellmann and Luke Gibbons.

Lectures at the University of Durham, Brown University, and the University of South Carolina provided very useful forums for feedback on the work in progress. I owe a debt of thanks to Michelle Clayton.

My partner and polestar Ludovico Geymonat has shared the whole life of this book and contributed to it in countless ways.

My parents, Carmel and Colin, my brother Killian, along with many friends and extended family, weave a web of safety and affection that gives a meaning to all endeavors.

I dedicate the book to Caitríona Ní Dhúill, whose wholly original spirit is a light in my life and illuminates many of these pages, and to my brother Ronan, with whom I share more than one private language. Thanks to both of them for all the things, old and new, they share with me: *bíonn an siúlach scéalach*.

LANGUAGES OF THE NIGHT

INTRODUCTION:
THE GREAT SILENCE IN CARROWLIAM BEG

In an article recalling how it came to be that he did not inherit what he considered to be a fully native command of Irish, Ó Ríordáin described the linguistic shift in his own townland of Gortnatubbrid on the Cork-Kerry border as follows:

> Irish was retreating into the night. It was mostly at night that you would hear the Irish of the old people, and you associated the language with the night.
> [bhí an Ghaeilge ag cúladh isteach san oíche. Istoíche isea is mó a chloisfeá Gaeilge na seandaoine, agus is leis an oíche a shamhlófí an teanga.][1]

My book takes its title from this comment of Ó Ríordáin's, and its origins are in my own memories of someone very old. My great-grandmother, Annie Meehan, née Hegarty, died at the age of ninety-seven, when I was ten. She was from the townland of Carrowliam Beg, in a district on the eastern edges of County Mayo called Tumgesh, still pronounced *Thoom-yesh* according to its original Irish name, *Tuaim Gheis*. She spent almost her whole life in the vicinity of Tumgesh, and it is where her daughter, my grandmother Kathleen, was also born and reared. I remember my great-grandmother as a tougher, more concentrated version of my grandmother, as someone for whom the supernatural world of saints and blessings had an alarming immediacy. The last time I saw her she was lying in bed with her arms outstretched, declaring that she saw the gates of heaven opening before her, not in the prayerful tones of a dutiful parishioner, but with the passionate possession of a shaman.

As is the habit with these strong family figures after they die, there were certain things that it became routine, almost ritualistic to say about her: she considered green an unlucky color, and hawthorn—"the devil's bread"—an unlucky flower; she attributed her longevity to the drinking of cabbage-water; she was fond of brandy and of silvermints. Something else that was often repeated in the family about her, as though it was an eccentricity of the same kind, was that she "knew no Irish." In retrospect it is odd that this should have been considered worthy of comment. In the 1980s, the language had been compulsory in the Irish education system for some sixty years, but with mixed results. It was a language we almost never encountered outside school; not everyone had had a long or a successful education, and so knowing or not knowing Irish was hardly a memorable or a distinguishing characteristic.

The first hint that there was something else hidden inside this oft-repeated but apparently futile fact is that it was usually accompanied by another one, which was that even though my great-grandmother could not speak or understand Irish, her English was peppered with individual Irish words and phrases. She knew these only phonetically, and they were usually words or expressions unfamiliar to the kind of Irish we had all learned at school. One word was *taca*, which meant something like a wallflower at a party (it appears in Dinneen's dictionary meaning a "prop"). Another was *marbh fháisc air*, "may he die by choking," a curse so malignant she would only utter it in a whisper.

More peculiarly, Annie was remembered as jokingly reciting a single phrase: *coicís go mbeidh sí ag teacht*, "she will be coming in a fortnight's time." This last chunk of phonetic Irish was a humorous imitation Annie was said to have enjoyed doing of an old neighbor of hers "long ago." Who this neighbor was, who was coming to visit her, and, more interestingly, why she announced it in Irish to my great-grandmother who could not speak the language, were questions not addressed in this frequently retold yet mysteriously empty story. Only recently, a longer version of it resurfaced in the family. The phrase had been uttered by an older woman who lived next door and whose son had recently married; the impending arrival was of the new daughter-in-law, who was preparing to move in. Dreading her certain fate as a useless old woman relegated to the dark corners of her own cottage, she had wanted to "vent" in private, and spoke

2

the phase in Irish to my great-grandmother so that the children in the room—my grandmother and her two sisters—would not understand. The joke of the story was that, while my great-grandmother, who did not know Irish at all, registered *coicís go mbeidh sí ag teacht* as incomprehensible gibberish, her daughters, from whom it was supposed to be concealed, were studying Irish in school and knew exactly what it meant.

Many mysterious things remain about these memories: why so many of the few stories repeated about my great-grandmother, a hardy, practical woman of the land, seem to touch on the question of language; why her next-door neighbor spoke Irish but my great-grandmother did not; what was so interesting or shocking in the neighbor's confusion about who would or wouldn't understand Irish; most of all, why this seemingly trivial fragment of a memory was considered to be a story at all, let alone one that was remembered and passed down in such a reduced, stunted form, for a hundred years.

Freudian dream analysis distinguishes between "manifest content" and "latent content." The manifest content of stories that appear to have no meaning or seem truncated in some way yet are passed down and retold through generations often hide latent content, from origins in a lost set of events that are hard or traumatic to narrate directly. And so I think it must be with this story. We know astonishingly little about the lived experience of language change in nineteenth-century Ireland or about what kinds of bilingualism persisted as it happened. It must have been chaotic, and for many people it must have been a defining feature of their lifetimes, yet as to how this change occurred and what it was like to be caught in the midst of it, we are faced with, in the memorable phrase of Seán de Fréine, a "great silence." Not only does language change receive only the most cursory mention in histories of Ireland—even social histories of Ireland[2]—it is rarely even part of the discourse of language revivalism, which has taken the colonial battle between Irish-speaking Ireland and English-speaking occupiers as its central focus and has given scant attention to the internal dynamics of language shift. There are well-documented incidents of monoglot Irish speakers being denied a fair trial—recounted

3

in Joyce's essay "Ireland at the Bar"—and we know that the practice of children being beaten at school for speaking Irish was widespread (using methods partly devised and implemented by Irish speakers themselves, also common in other minor-language situations such as Wales, Scotland, and Provence),[3] but astoundingly few stories have come down to us of linguistic conflict or complications within the Irish communities themselves as they moved from one language to another.[4]

The weirdly inconsequential anecdote about my great-grandmother Annie and her neighbor may be a version of what Freud called "screen memories," one apparently harmless but puzzling story standing in for another that is too big or troubling to look at. It strikes me that within the *coicís* story lurks a reality never otherwise mentioned: that two languages coexisted in Tumgesh during my great-grandmother's lifetime (and into my grandmother's childhood), and that there was some confusion about who spoke which, even when it was a question of close neighbors. The obvious place to seek more background is the census figures. A census question on the Irish language has been asked since 1851, providing, as Pádraig Ó Riagáin points out, "one of the oldest continuous series of regularly collected, standard public statistics on any language in the world."[5] When applied to wide geographical areas, to the country or to whole counties, the statistics tell us, alas, very little. It is evident from many returns that individuals and families described themselves as either bilingual or speakers of Irish only out of patriotism or wishful thinking. In addition, in the pre-1926 censuses, the language question was confusingly phrased on the form, and seems to have led to a great deal of uncertainty and error.[6] The aggregate census figures cannot tell us anything about what language change felt like, how it manifested itself in daily life; and what is more constitutive of daily life than the language one speaks to one's parents, children, and, indeed, neighbors?

If, however, we scrutinize the census returns for Carrowliam Beg in 1901, compiled when Annie was fifteen, and 1911, when she was twenty-five, the numbers show that during Annie's childhood

Tumgesh and Carrowliam Beg were in the throes of an astonishingly rapid linguistic transition. I never heard anything about my great-grandmother's parents, my great-great grandparents, other than that they had grown up in the same stretch of country on the Mayo-Sligo border. In both the census of 1901 and that of 1911 my great-grandmother can be found still living at home with them. Under the section "Irish language" Annie's parents are returned as speakers of "Irish and English," while my great-grandmother and her sisters are all listed as speaking "English only." The same holds for her future husband, my great-grandfather, living at home with his bilingual, illiterate, widowed mother a few miles away (intriguingly, the 1901 census records my great-grandfather, then seventeen, and all his siblings, as speaking both Irish and English, but in 1911 as speaking English only).[7]

Since they could not have acquired Irish at school, my great-grandmother's parents were certainly native speakers of Irish. They must have made a concerted effort to prevent their children from learning their shared mother tongue. The scraps of Irish that littered my great-grandmother's speech must have fallen into it despite their best efforts, the result of an English learned from people for whom it was a foreign language. They were fragments left over from a world that had disappeared during her youth, the last, stubborn shards of a lost, vernacular form of Irish that, after more than a thousand years, had suddenly receded from east Mayo when she was a girl.

In 1901, when Annie was seventeen, out of the total population of 159 in Carrowliam Beg, just over half (eighty-seven people) are recorded on the census as bilingual. Seventy-one individuals, including Annie, could speak only English. Far more telling is the age distribution of these groups. In 1901, there is no one over the age of thirty-three in Carrowliam Beg who cannot speak Irish, but a mere handful under twenty who can. There is one seventy-year-old woman, Catherine Grady, who can speak only Irish. Does her ghost lie behind the stubborn persistence of the *coicís* half anecdote? Does the story of the neighbor who was counting down the days till she would be cast into irrelevance within her own home by a young new arrival, unconsciously articulate the trauma of mass language change otherwise hidden under a "great silence"? Does it also record the predicament of a different Irish-speaking neighbor, Catherine Grady, suddenly thrown into the linguistic and social night of her own community?

As far as I (or any of my relatives who remember her) can tell, my great-grandmother never mentioned that anyone in Carrowliam Beg when she was growing up spoke Irish at all, ever, except for this memory of the single neighbor and her anxious phrase, let alone that it was the language her parents had grown up in. Yet when we consider that this was a small, interdependent community of only one hundred and fifty people, the linguistic divide between the old and the young must have been a striking feature of life in Carrowliam Beg at the turn of the last century.[8]

The census figures show that not knowing Irish was unheard of in Tumgesh at the time of my great-grandmother's birth. Her own parents must have grown up in a thoroughly Irish-speaking world. Their own parents likely knew English poorly, at best; they themselves must have courted and farmed and cut turf in Irish, they may have whispered it to each other out of the children's earshot, or continued to use it with elderly relatives and neighbors whose English was weak. My great-grandmother might well have had no language in common with her own grandparents.[9] What this must have been like for them, or what it must have been like for Catherine Grady, living a few doors away and still wholly enclosed in the mental bubble of the lost vernacular, is difficult to imagine: having lived all of their lives in the same place, spoken the language of its place-names and history, having spoken, indeed, a micro-dialect of the language unique to the townland itself, and connected intimately and inseparably from its landscape and memories, they found themselves foreigners at home, surrounded on all sides by an alien language, unable to speak to their own young neighbors. This is a relatively common experience for immigrant families, but an even stranger one for people who had never left the place they were from.

One of the few eyewitness accounts we do have about how this process occurred comes from an area not far from Tumgesh. Fr. Tomás Ó Ceallaigh, a priest on the border between Sligo and Roscommon, gave an account of the language change in his district, in which he says that everyone over sixty had spoken nothing but Irish in their childhood and had learned English at school with the encouragement of their parents, who themselves knew little or no English:

> When these people married they taught their children not the old speech that was as honey on their lips, but the English which with so much pain they had acquired. They had been brought up in the belief that English was the top-notch of respectability, the key that opened Sesame, and they were determined that their children should not be left without a boon so precious. Prayers which they had never quite learned in English (some of them pray in Irish to the present day) were continued in Irish in their homes; apart from that, Irish was to their children an esoteric speech employed by their elders to express things not meant for their ears. The children then grew up ignorant of any language but English; at home or in school they never heard anything else with the unimportant exception I have just noted.[10]

As the people of Tumgesh and other places like it were deliberately, and likely with great difficulty, preventing the transmission of Irish to the next generation, in Dublin and other towns, the Gaelic League, devoted to the preservation and propagation of the language, was gaining popularity and political power. My grandmother, Annie's daughter Kathleen, was born in Tumgesh in 1917, just six years after the 1911 census records a substantially bilingual population. Yet she never, as far as I can tell, encountered a native speaker from the locality, nor seemed to have any sense that anything other than English had been spoken there in living memory. My grandmother thought of herself as a product of an English-speaking place, and she considered the Gaeltacht, the collective term for those districts where Irish survived as the native language, as a distinct and distant cultural region, even a strange one, separate in vernacular, culture, and customs from her part of the country.

In the Tumgesh of my great-grandmother's youth, abandoning Irish for English was a symbol and means of progress and educational advancement; Irish was something that had always sprouted naturally in the locality, a sign of a traumatic past that had to be deliberately eradicated in order to move forward.[11] For my grandmother, on the other hand, born less than thirty years later, Tumgesh was a naturally English-speaking place, and for her Irish was a serious school subject, the official language of the state, a badge of education and a key to securing employment in its bureaucracy. She worked hard at Irish and was proud to have mastered it, but I almost never heard her speak it. Irish was for her a mute, high language, a badge of officialdom and patriotic ideals, a sign of education. It was spoken as a vernacular, exceptionally so, by the fishermen of Connemara and west Kerry—places one was sent to perfect one's command of the language—but for everyone else, it was a tongue of solemn national pronouncements, ceremonies, and official certificates or prizes. Her own mother's ignorance of Irish was a sign of old-fashionedness and an educational lack. For my grandmother, Irish was not connected with her native east Mayo, or to her own grandparents, but to a linguistic elsewhere, simultaneously in the past and the future.[12]

Who knows what my great-grandmother, whose own parents and their generation had gone to such lengths to prevent her becoming an Irish speaker, at a time when native Irish, if you had gone looking for it, was in such abundance, made of her own daughters spending their precious education toiling away at Irish grammar, at prepositional pronouns, dependent verb forms, eclipsis, and lenition, learning from textbooks that *coicís* means "fortnight." Whether the sound of it reminded her of her old neighbors or of private conversations between her parents, we do not know. But she must have registered the way in which the ghost of Irish from her own or her parents' past coincided with the modern dream of the Irish of the national future she saw in the schooling of her children and grandchildren, and surely must have been struck, after all the painful, traumatizing efforts that had gone into the creation of her own generation's

8

English monolingualism, by the amount of effort, a mere generation later, that was now devoted to acquiring Irish again.[13]

Or was it "again"? Were they relearning the same language that their own great-grandparents had, if we take Fr. Ó Ceallaigh's description, so deliberately extinguished? Is the vernacular my great-grandmother must have heard, at least occasionally, perhaps at night, in the chatting of older neighbors in Carrowliam Beg—which must have seemed to them far from honey on their lips—the same language as the state-sponsored, dutiful Irish, studied, taught, printed on signs and forms in independent Ireland but rarely heard in spontaneous interactions in daily life? Language only becomes "honey" on lips of its natives once it is endangered. Two Irishes co-incided and collided in Carrowliam Beg in the first decades of the twentieth century, a ghost of Irish past and a dream of Irish future. The ghost was the still fresh but quickly fading memory of the language that had been the medium of life in the townland for many centuries, now cast into the shameful oblivion of the night (and pre-served in fossilized fragments in my great-grandmother's English). The dream was that of the first official language of a newly indepen-dent Irish state, looking forward to its future among the nations of the world.

These speculations on the experience of language change in a place like Tumgesh can be extended to the literary psychology of language. As Irish was found less and less "in the wild," this book will argue, it acquired unusual potential properties for the poetic imagination, as a dream of another, lost, more perfect language hidden beneath the surface of English-speaking Ireland. There is no doubt that the desire to revive Irish comes in part from a longing to repair broken links with the past, to restore something old rather than to create something new. But the underlying meaning the language acquired as it was spoken less as a native language, as a troubling ghost haunt-ing everyday life in English-speaking Ireland, is inseparable from the modernist literary ideas that had such a hold on early twentieth-century Irish writers.

Few scholars of modernist European literature pay much attention to minor languages, other than an obligatory postcolonial nod to the passage in Joyce's *A Portrait of the Artist as a Young Man* where Stephen Dedalus reflects on his soul fretting in the shadow of English. Only in Ireland, where the language movement was a major ideological component of a successful political struggle, has the experience of mass language change been understood as a formative part of its cultural destiny. But Ireland has always considered its experience of vernacular shift to have been a unique phenomenon that sets it apart from all other European nations (even from its cousins on the Celtic fringes of the United Kingdom and France). There are some reasons, which we shall explore in later chapters, why the case of the Irish language does present some unique features. But the Irish are not the only European people to fret in the shadow of a lost language. There were versions of Tumgesh all over western Europe in the early twentieth century, and from them sprang a change in the feeling of what language meant that was, this book will argue, at the heart of modernist writing.

Language Loss in Twentieth-Century Western Europe

In the same decade that Annie Meehan's neighbor in Carrowliam Beg tried to use Irish as a secret code to tell my great-grandmother about her fears, in Paris Marcel Proust wrote a scene in in *La Prisonnière*, the fifth volume of the *Recherche*, in which the narrator's housekeeper, Françoise, and her daughter speak the local dialect to one another in front of him so that he cannot understand what they are saying. The narrator notices that the two women only speak their native language (a local dialect of the Eure-et-Loir, where the fictional Combray is situated) as a secret argot to exclude him. Once the narrator becomes familiar with their patois and it can no longer serve this pragmatic purpose, he tells us, they abandon it altogether and thenceforth speak together only in French.

The shift in the speech of country people from minor languages such as Irish or local varieties such as Françoise's patois to metropolitan standards like English or French was one of the most notable and immediate cultural elements of "modernity" in Europe during the flowering and aftermath of modernist writing. The postcolonial attention to the ways in which European languages supplanted or repressed indigenous speech forms abroad has partly caused scholars to overlook the diversity of linguistic experiences within the borders of the colonizing European powers themselves. But another reason the dramatic demise of rural speech varieties in twentieth-century Europe has not received more comparative attention is that official, metropolitan cultures have had such differing views of the meaning of linguistic change, from Ireland, where the restoration of Irish was for many years the "first official aim" of the government, to France, where until well into the twentieth century the extinction of all speech forms other than French was part of government policy. It is worth taking a moment to give a brief overview of the sociolinguistic history of some of the major western European countries.

If nationalist sentiment, as we shall see, has contributed to an overstatement of the extent to which vernacular Irish has survived in Ireland, the same patriotic loyalty in France historically led to a deliberate understatement of the use of local dialects and regional languages.[14] In literary terms, the rise of the standard of Île-de-France was early and comprehensive. From the sixteenth century on, apart from sporadic Occitan movements and other minor exceptions, in France, unlike Italy or Germany, there was little literary activity in dialects. As W. Theodor Elwert points out, even in French adaptations of the commedia dell'arte, which in Italy always involved characters speaking dialect (Arlecchino traditionally spoke Bergamasque, for example), or in French burlesque drama, which employed all other sorts of puns and wordplay, dialect words rarely appear.[15] Moreover, French Romanticism was unusual in that it did not engender an interest in the rural languages and dialects of France. Even in French-speaking Switzerland, French was never challenged as a literary standard.

At the same time, this intense literary standardization had relatively little effect on the ordinary speech of the countryside until the mid-nineteenth century; one of the chief failures of the Napoleonic education system was considered to be that it did not succeed in eradicating local languages and dialects.[16] As Martin Lyons points out, "For millions of French citizens, the French Revolution was conducted in a foreign language."[17] Historically, the educated, the wealthy, and city dwellers spoke French, but they were a minority of the population; most people else spoke dialects particular to their own small communities.[18] As late as the end of the nineteenth century, the period in which Proust's novel is set, a large proportion of the French population still did not consider themselves speakers of French. When the Blessed Virgin appeared to Berndadette Soubirous in Lourdes in 1858, she proclaimed the doctrine of the Immaculate Conception to her in Bernadette's native language, Gascon: *Que soy era immaculada concepciou*. Gascon was the language spoken day in, day out by Bernadette and her community. We think of her as a French saint, but French was far from her world: it was a language spoken far off in the north of France or in the big towns, used in rural Gascony only in official or formal contexts that had little bearing on the daily experience of a miller's daughter like Bernadette.

Yet from the end of the century onward, the disappearance of both patois and regional languages was extraordinarily swift and complete. In 1901, most people living in lower Brittany could not speak French; fifty years later, Breton was spoken in only the most remote places, and native intergenerational transmission had collapsed. The same applies to the other languages and dialects that had been in vigorous spoken use in France until then. Across the south, speakers of the Occitan dialects, the vernacular descendants of the literary language of the Troubadours, turned en masse to French; Nissart, the once-flourishing dialect of Nice, the Gallo-Italic dialect of Corsica, and, most dramatically of all, the spectrum of patois that had been the ordinary speech of rural people across northern and central France, all fell rapidly out of use in the first half of the twentieth century. In 1999, no less than 90 percent of adult men whose fathers had usually spoken to them in Francoprovençal in their childhoods did not do likewise with their own children—a near-total linguistic collapse in a single generation.[19] The mass retreat and even extinction of all of these linguistic varieties might seem not to have impinged on French metropolitan literary culture at all; as we shall see in the chapter on Proust, this is far from being the case.[20]

Britain presents a different situation again. Other than in Scotland, regional dialects of English also perished early as literary mediums. According to Elwert, dialects fell out of written use in England between the fifteenth and seventeenth centuries.[21] In Britain's Celtic-speaking periphery, however, the early twentieth century saw a dramatic shift to the use of English as vernacular. The Cornish language had already become defunct as a native language by the end of the eighteenth century, but Manx, the Gaelic language of the Isle of Man went with great rapidity from being the ordinary language of the island in the mid-nineteenth century to becoming extinct as a mother tongue in the twentieth, its last native speaker dying in 1974.[22] In Wales, 80 percent of the population was Welsh-speaking as the nineteenth century opened, most of them unable to speak English; by the beginning of the twentieth, the proportion had almost halved, and more than 90 percent of the population could speak English. The proportion of Welsh speakers was to halve again over the next sixty years. These numbers were partly due to population increase in parts of Wales that were English-speaking already, but by the 1950s the traditional Welsh-speaking heartland itself had begun to contract and fragment as Welsh-speaking communities themselves abandoned their language for English.[23] In Scotland, there were a quarter of a million native Gaelic speakers in 1891; one hundred years later, there were sixty thousand, and the language remained in use as a vernacular only in the Hebrides and other far western pockets[24] (Hugh MacDiarmid's modernist invention of a synthetic version of Scots English might have offered an interesting parallel for Ó Ríordáin or Pasolini, but at the time MacDiarmid was writing, Scots was vernacular throughout much of Scotland and thus presents a somewhat distinct case).

In southern Germany, Austria, and Switzerland, local dialects retained to some extent their place as a language of home and village. But during the population upheavals of the two world wars and their aftermath, northern Germany saw an enormous falling-off in the use of Low German dialects (*Plattdeutsch*). At the outbreak of the First World War, these dialects had been the near-universal language of home and colloquial interactions outside of the middle and upper classes; by the 1960s, they had been to a great degree supplanted by High German.[25]

In Spain, the Reconquest and internal migrations left the peninsula early on with less dialect variation than its Romance-speaking neighbors, and, outside Catalonia, Galicia and the Basque Country, standard Castilian established itself early as a mass vernacular in rural Spain, even beyond Castile proper. The Spanish dialects of Asturias, Aragon, and Extremadura all suffered a dramatic reduction in use in the twentieth century, especially after the Civil War. Catalan held its own as the language of the mercantile classes of Catalonia, so is not considered a minor language for our purposes here, and Galician, or Gallego, closely related to Portuguese, remained in widespread use. Basque, however, whose territory had been shrinking since the nineteenth century, suffered an accelerated decline after the Second World War, though it has retained its position as the dominant home language in its north-central heartlands in the provinces of Bizkaia and Gipuzkoa, and has consolidated its position in recent decades.

White Martyrdom

The conviction that one's mother tongue, one's national language, the language one employs in intimate relationships, and the language of poetry ought to be the same is a relatively new one in Europe, ultimately traceable, perhaps, to the Romantic idea that poetry was the expression of an individual soul through which also spoke the soul of an identifiable collective—often national—community. This conviction was an impulse both for the modern evolution of lyric poetry and for the ethnographic efforts of the nineteenth century, which devoted the first serious attention to the languages spoken by the European peasantry (and to their songs and folklore). The quasi-mystical idea of language as a pure expression of both an individual and a collective identity was one of the central elements behind the "discovery"—especially, but by no means only, in Ireland—and sacralization of "popular" folk culture in rural languages.

As part of a general wave of curiosity about and often exaltation of these folk cultures, minor languages and local dialects had already sparked the interest of the folkloric Romanticism and philological enthusiasm of the nineteenth century. The Grimms undertook close analysis of German dialects, and Napoleonic France commissioned a comprehensive survey of the "parlers et patois" spoken throughout France, albeit with the express purpose of exterminating (*anéantir*) them. Then, however, these forms of language were still a part of daily reality, something one could take for granted in much of Europe outside big towns. The modernist rediscovery of these languages and dialects that is the subject of *Languages of the Night* is something quite different, the result of their decline (or of the prospect of their decline) as mass vernaculars. As they fell out of wide spoken use, or threatened to do so, they became associated with a lost, unrecoverable, intimate relationship to language itself.

The decline in native, spoken use of minor languages has often been accompanied or followed by a burst of literary activity by non-native speakers (not all of it by any means modernist in character). Each language community seems to have viewed this apparently cruel coincidence of literary renaissance and vernacular collapse as a private curse or inexplicable irony of its own making. Franco Brevini marveled at the contradictory situation whereby the Italian dialects were undergoing "an unforeseen poetic renewal coinciding with the most serious crisis that the dialects have ever experienced at the level of [spoken] usage."[26] Peredur Lynch similarly remarks with regard to the decline of vernacular Welsh: "That Welsh literature should have flourished in such a context is . . . a perplexing paradox."[27] In France, Francis Favereau wonders at the same contradiction in modern Breton literature: "By the 1950s . . . most parents had turned to French as the main medium of communication with their children. . . . Paradoxically, the twentieth century has been, on the whole, the most productive ever for Breton literature."[28]

The fact that this paradox is remarked on with such astonishment in so many different minor-language situations in Europe suggests that it may not be a coincidence. These belated bursts of poetry do not usually, despite the hopes of revivalists, represent a new lease of life for an old tradition but are rather the result of particular poetic properties generated or released precisely by the fact or, more often, prospect of a language's demise in the sphere of spontaneous speech or community life. The possibility of a language's disappearance allows it to become a carrier for a variety of other frustrations and longings. In the end, the truth may be that the poet and the revivalist, the artist and the linguist, may not have the same interests. Both may secretly reside in the same person—lamenting decline, longing for renewal, but ultimately inspired by the poetic possibilities of vernacular death.[29]

Before the eighteenth century it was relatively common to write in a language other than the one one spoke in everyday conversation, and indeed to write in a language that in a vernacular sense was dead. This is true not only of the Latin of the Humanists but also for many other cases, such as French writers brought up in communities that spoke local dialects, or (as to this day) in Luxembourg and in German-speaking Switzerland. But the practice with which we will be concerned here, of deliberately adopting a minor, rural vernacular language and reshaping it into a unique medium of poetry, is something quite different.

In what is perhaps the best-known theoretical work on minor literature, *Kafka: Toward a Minor Literature*, Gilles Deleuze and Félix Guattari state that, by definition, a minor literature cannot be produced in a minor language but "is rather that which a minority constructs within a major language."[30] For Deleuze and Guattari "the first characteristic of minor literature . . . is that in it language is affected with a high coefficient of deterritorialization." Deleuze and Guattari's thoughts here are shaped by an unspoken and erroneous assumption: that a minor language is always the mother tongue, the home vernacular, either bound to a specific territory (like Czech) or "oral and popular" (like Yiddish). As long as minor languages and dialects remain the vernacular of their communities, there is some truth in this assumption. But this is not the reality for languages and dialects whose vernacular use declined over the course of the twentieth century, and which were repurposed as literary mediums for writers reared in major languages. Deleuze and Guattari's assumption is that minor languages are the native tongue of writers from linguistic minorities, who forsake its familiarity and comfort for an alien and hostile major language. But the reverse phenomenon, the white martyrdom of moving from major to minor, represents a more extreme "coefficient of deterriorialization."[31]

At one of the many moments in *Finnegans Wake* when Joyce's text talks about itself, it describes a "Nichtian glossery . . . which is nat language at any sinse of the world." *Nicht* and *nat* are both words for "night" (Scots and Danish, respectively). The language of the *Wake*, this is to say, is a not-language and a night-language, a language that cannot be found in ordinary, waking life but that has been retrieved from the darkness beyond or below the daily, visible world. This could serve of a description of the way Ó Ríordáin used Irish and Pasolini used Friulian. In neither case was it a language they had grown up speaking at home, nor the language that came to them most naturally, but a language that corresponded to an inner, solitary, lyric vision. Ó Ríordáin and Pasolini were writing poetry in Irish and Friulian within just a few years of *Finnegans Wake*, and their adoption and transformation of minor, rural languages as personal poetic idioms constitutes a singular form, in itself, of modernist expression. Nonnative speakers of their chosen minor languages, both Ó Ríordáin and Pasolini longingly admire the for them unachievable naturalness of native speech. This is not, however, an exaltation of a nation or a home, as one would find in Romanticism, but rather an expression of homelessness, of existential exile.

In the early Irish monastic church, being killed for one's religion was known as "red martyrdom." "White martyrdom," *bán-martra*, on the other hand, was to go into exile from one's homeland and community, described (in what is the oldest extant sermon in Old Irish) thus: "This is white martyrdom to a man: when he renounces everything he loves for God [Is í an bán-martra do dhuine, an tan scaras, as son Dé, re gach rud a charas]."[32] We might think of the decision by poets to write in a minor language that was never their mother tongue, forsaking the comfort, familiarity, and indeed readership of their native major language to do so, as a form of literary white martyrdom. Both Ó Ríordáin and Pasolini forsook the ease and possible readership they might have enjoyed had they written in their mother tongues, English and Italian (Pasolini indeed went on to do so), with no real alternative audience to address instead. Certainly not the rural communities for whom Irish and Friulian were still a mother tongue, since both poets wrote in synthetic, semi-invented versions of their chosen languages that no native speaker could identify with.[33] Eliot's *The Waste Land*, with all its untranslated fragments of Sanskrit, Greek, Old Provençal, and so on, Pound's *Cantos*, or, most of all, Joyce's *Wake* itself, written in its own invented superlanguage, are built around an imaginary, utopian conception of a reader that does not correspond with anyone who could be found in the real world. Rather than reviving or renewing a dormant tradition, Ó Ríordáin exploited Irish, and Pasolini Friulian, to generate readymade, private languages of art, invented, personal poetic idioms whose literary power depended on their decline (or the prospect of it) as spoken mediums of daily life.

When he was compiling his *Linguistic Atlas and Survey of Irish Dialects* between 1949 and 1953, the Swiss linguist Heinrich Wagner scoured the Irish countryside looking for surviving native speakers of the Irish language in the parts of the country where the language was almost extinct (including a district close to Tumgesh). In the preface to his results he wrote: "We are not dealing with a language spoken over a wide area but rather with the ruins of a language. We compare our work with the archaeologist's task of reconstructing an old building from a heap of stones, lying here and there in the place where the original building stood."[34] For Wagner, a philologist, this situation was obviously to be bitterly regretted; he lamented the fact that he had not conducted his survey only a decade or two earlier, when the extent and quality of information he could have gathered would have been so much richer. Wagner saw in these ruins the tragic signs of death, demise, and loss. This book is about the very different imaginative possibilities offered to the literary imagination by these ruins, possibilities that flourishing, widely spoken languages cannot offer: a privileged glimpse into the limits and failures of language, but also into the nature of the utopian hopes we nonetheless place in it.

LANGUAGE ~~one~~ OF THE DEAD:
THE IRISH LANGUAGE IN THE TWENTIETH CENTURY

"The language that my soul speaks is . . . Irish."
—Nuala Ní Dhomhnaill, "Why I Choose to Write in
Irish, the Corpse That Sits Up and Talks Back"

"—Well, said Gabriel, if it comes to that, you
know, Irish is not my language."
—James Joyce, "The Dead"

James Joyce and the Irish Language

We can find something of a resonance with my great-grandmother's fragment of Irish, in "Eveline," a story in James Joyce's *Dubliners*. On her deathbed, the senile mother of the eponymous protagonist repeats the words "derevaun seraun, derevaun seraun" (p. 33), apparently meaningless babble that haunts Eveline for the rest of her days.[1] There is no doubt, from the rhythm of the words, and from the common Irish suffix "-aun" (*-án*) that it was Joyce's intention to make these words mimic the sound of Irish; whether it is pretend Irish as invented in a state of dementia by a non-Irish speaker, or a genuine scrap of Irish distorted in phonetic rendering by the hearer (in this case the daughter listening at the bedside), we do not know.[2] We do know that Joyce's knowledge of Irish was limited, and therefore that if he had wanted to include real Irish words he would have had to rely on an Irish-speaking informant (as he did for words in *Finnegans Wake*). But, although they sound like Irish, the words "derevaun seraun" do not correspond to any actual words in the language. The many attempts in Joyce scholarship to ascribe real Gaelic meanings to them have been fanciful or ill-informed.[3] Attempts to trace them back to a meaningful phrase in the language is futile for a good reason: the point of the phrase is its lack of meaning. They are a fragment of a lost language and lost world, unmotivated signs that cannot signify in the world they find themselves in. Whatever reality in which they might have had meaning—a vanished historical past when the forgotten language was a vernacular, or the distorted, equally unreachable mental landscape of a senile mind—is gone. They are the form of Irish stripped of its content, representing a pure, radical language loss.

As my great-grandmother's story shows, Irish was spoken more widely as a vernacular in the nineteenth century than we might imagine from surviving accounts. Given how common native Irish still was in the second half of the nineteenth century, many of the older characters in *Dubliners* would have to have had memories of relatives or older acquaintances whose daily language was or had been Irish. As we shall see, the phrase pronounced by Molly Ivors in "The Dead" shows the emergent Gaelic revival movement entering the consciousness of middle-class, English-speaking Dublin, but these words in "Eveline" are traces of an earlier phenomenon, the disappearance of the language as a native vernacular from most of the country. The words do not stand for any specific memory of the language, or at least not one that we can access, but are a way of registering that faded remnants of vernacular Irish must have been one of the many strands, even if a faint one, running through the collective psychology of Edwardian Dublin.

The turnaround between the abandonment of Irish as a vernacular and the sacralization of the language as the lost tongue of the nation's soul was rapid. Subsequent appearances of Irish in Joyce, other than in the *Wake*, have to do with the later question of revivalism, when native spoken Irish, far from being an unremarkable part of rural life or of folk memory, had been invested with imaginative and symbolic meanings. After "Eveline," Irish makes its appearance in Joyce's work mostly as an idea rather than as a language. In the opening chapter of *Ulysses*, when Joyce is announcing the shape of his epic, for example, he makes Haines, an arrogant and clueless Englishman, the mouthpiece of the language revival. In the first pages of the chapter, Buck Mulligan had mocked the Latin mass. The first lines of dialogue spoken in *Ulysses*, "Introibo ad altare Dei" (1.05), are in Latin, a language that is no longer a vernacular; this blasphemous "mass," which Mulligan enacts in their lodgings using a shaving bowl instead of a chalice, brings up the question of how language and myth are related to everyday life.

An exchange a few pages later about the Irish language can be read in the same vein, as designed to emphasize the fact that Irish, at least in the society where *Ulysses* takes place, is not the language of the common people. In this incident, the three men in the tower—Stephen, Mulligan, and Haines—are visited by the local milk woman. Haines, a Gaelic enthusiast from England, naïvely assumes that, by virtue of being an agricultural worker, she must be an Irish speaker. Since they are in the southern suburbs of Dublin, a place that had not been Irish-speaking for many centuries, this is an absurdly ignorant assumption. The ensuing dialogue ruthlessly drives home the fact that in this society Irish is not a vernacular, and at the same time strips the language of the mystical properties attributed to it by revivalism.

A canny financial operator, the milk woman cravenly praises Irish because she suspects it might ingratiate her with the men and perhaps encourage them to pay her the money she is owed. The exchange suggests that English, the living, "fallen" vernacular of Ireland, the venal language of the marketplace rather than that of the eternal spirit, is a source of vitality, if also of commerce:

> —Is it French you are talking, sir? the old woman said to Haines.
> Haines spoke to her again a longer speech, confidently.
> —Irish, Buck Mulligan said. Is there Gaelic on you?
> —I thought it was Irish, she said, by the sound of it. Are you from the west, sir?
> —I am an Englishman, Haines answered.
> —He's English, Buck Mulligan said, and he thinks we ought to speak Irish in Ireland.

—Sure we ought to, the old woman said, and I'm ashamed I don't
speak the language myself. I'm told it's a grand language by them that
knows.
—Grand is no name for it, said Buck Mulligan. Wonderful entirely.
(1.425–435)

The disconnection between Irish and vernacular speech is further
emphasized by the fact that the syntax of both the milk woman—
"Is it French you are talking?"—and Mulligan—"Is there Gaelic
on you?"—are classic examples of the Gaelic-influenced vernacular
English of Ireland: Irish is present as a ghost in English. The foreign-
ness of Irish to everyday life in Ireland, its inability to produce lived
dialogue and interaction, appears in other places in Joyce's work, too:
Molly scribbles random signs on a piece of paper and pretends they
are Irish script; Stephen sings a song in Irish to an uncomprehending
Bloom, one of the hints of failed communication in their encounter;
in the "Cyclops" episode, the citizen, the most damning portrayal
of a Gaelic Leaguer, speaks Irish chiefly to his dog, while the dialogue among the men in the pub is another tour-de-force rendering
of Hiberno-English; in *A Portrait of the Artist as a Young Man*, when
Mulrennan goes on a trip to the Irish-speaking West, the result of his
linguistic interaction with the native speakers is that "old man spoke
Irish. Mulrennan spoke Irish. Then old man and Mulrennan spoke
English" (pp. 254–255).

In "The Dead," the last story in *Dubliners*, however, Joyce gives
Gaelic revivalism a more nuanced analysis. In this story, the utopian feelings engendered by a longing for the lost Irish-speaking
world make an explicit appearance. On one level, the inclusion of
a Gaelic Leaguer, Molly Ivors, as a character in "The Dead," and
of a testy exchange about the ideology of language revival between
Miss Ivors and Gabriel Conroy, the story's central protagonist, is
simply part of Joyce's desire to provide an encyclopedic snapshot of
the variety of political and cultural currents in the air at the time.
After a youthful moment of hesitation (including an aspirational self-
description in the 1901 census as an Irish speaker) Joyce was opposed

to the Gaelic revival and its language politics. Yet the revival movement, and the impulses behind it, play a key role in "The Dead" and in its treatment of the modernist crisis of faith in language and signification. One of the story's central preoccupations is the individual's relationship to language. A key problem in "The Dead" is the idea that body and soul do not speak the same language. The first line of the story, "Lily, the caretaker's daughter, was literally run off her feet"—frequently cited as the example par excellence of Joyce's radical version of free indirect discourse—immediately sets up the problem of a mismatch between language and the body. Almost immediately after this, Gabriel's attempt to engage Lily in conversation goes badly wrong; he asks her if she is getting married, and her answer, "the men that is nowadays is all palaver" once more puts bodies—"men"—and language—"palaver"—in opposition. The question of the gap between one's inner intentions and the words we rely on as a medium to transmit them to others preys on Gabriel's mind as he frets about the after-dinner speech he will have to give to the assembled company later in the evening: "He would fail with them just as he had failed with the girl in the pantry. He had taken up a wrong tone. His whole speech was a mistake from first to last, an utter failure" (p. 203). When he does make the speech, he refers explicitly—if formulaically—to his anxieties about the inadequacy of the language he has at his disposal to embody his thoughts, feelings, and intentions:

> —It has fallen to my lot this evening, as in years past, to perform a very pleasing task, but a task for which I am afraid my poor powers as a speaker are all too inadequate.
> —No, no! said Mr. Browne.
> —But, however that may be, I can only ask you tonight to take the will for the deed, and to lend me your attention for a few moments while I endeavour to express to you in words what my feelings are on this occasion. (p. 203)

Gabriel associates language here with the failure to translate will into deeds; he is reflecting on how one's inner self is not fully native to any language. The idea that one might have to learn one's own language had come up in an apparently different context earlier in the evening, during the dancing before dinner, when Gabriel had found himself involved in a heated discussion with his friend Molly Ivors, a member of the Gaelic League:

> [Miss Ivors] said suddenly:
> —O, Mr Conroy, will you come for an excursion to the Aran Isles this summer? We're going to stay there a whole month. It will be splendid out in the Atlantic. You ought to come. Mr Clancy is coming, and Mr Kilkelly and Kathleen Kearney. It would be splendid for Gretta too if she'd come. She's from Connacht, isn't she?
> —Her people are, said Gabriel shortly.
> —But you will come, won't you? said Miss Ivors, laying her warm hand eagerly on his arm.
> —The fact is, said Gabriel, I have just arranged to go—
> —Go where? asked Miss Ivors.
> —Well, you know, every year I go for a cycling tour with some fellows and so—
> —But where? asked Miss Ivors.
> —Well, we usually go to France or Belgium or perhaps Germany, said Gabriel awkwardly.
> —And why do you go to France and Belgium, said Miss Ivors, instead of visiting your own land?
> —Well, said Gabriel, it's partly to keep in touch with the languages and partly for a change.
> —And haven't you your own language to keep in touch with—Irish? asked Miss Ivors.
> —Well, said Gabriel, if it comes to that, you know, Irish is not my language. (pp. 189–190)

Gabriel's several linguistic frustrations throughout the evening suggest, however, that English may not be his language either. The anxiety and disappointment he suffers before and after his dinner-table speech come from his sense that the language he uses is inadequate to his thoughts, that it fails to carry the meanings and intentions he has in his heart; once embodied in language, his ideas fail and crumble.

In the final pages of the story, he suffers another, more acute sense of the impossibility of communication and communion, this time with his wife, whose inner mental world and past life in the west of Ireland seem as unreachable to Gabriel as the world of the dead. Before he falls asleep that night, Gabriel's mind turns to this and to the other painful failures of communication and connection he has experienced over the course of the evening. Miss Ivors's invitation to go to the west to learn Irish weaves itself through these regretful reflections:

> His soul had approached that region where dwell the vast hosts of the dead. He was conscious of, but could not apprehend, their wayward and flickering existence. His own identity was fading out into a grey impalpable world: the solid world itself, which these dead had one time reared and lived in, was dissolving and dwindling.
>
> A few light taps upon the pane made him turn to the window. It had begun to snow again. He watched sleepily the flakes, silver and dark, falling obliquely against the lamplight. The time had come for him to set out on his journey westward. (pp. 224–225)

Gabriel's epiphany is partly sparked by the conversation with Miss Ivors about where to go on holidays. By the end of the story, the Irish-speaking West has shifted from being a real place you can travel to and cycle through, where Miss Ivors is planning to go that summer with Mr. Clancy and Mr. Kilkelly and Kathleen Kearney, to being a mystical place where soul and body are at one. Gabriel does not seem likely to become a revivalist; he has been touched and challenged, not by Irish itself, but by the *dream* of Irish, by the vision of a distant western land where language and thought and feeling would be at one, where all conflict and loneliness would be resolved by the possibility of true communion with others.

The vision of the West that ends the story is the realm of the next world, "that region where dwell the vast hosts of the dead," but also a place where full connection with others—what has been so painfully impossible during the evening—would be possible. Irish in "The Dead," the language of "the West," is an imaginary or symbolic solution to the problem of how we are dead to each other and to ourselves, to the problem of failed embodied communication, the gap between words and feelings, soul and mind, the living and the dead. "The Dead" is a story about the tragic limitations of language, about how it fails to connect us, as we wish, to the souls of others, about how our own souls find themselves not at home in it. In the story, Joyce depicts (without embracing) the revivalist dream of Irish as a miraculous answer to these problems: an ideal of a lost, perfect language which would unite body and soul.

"The Dead" takes place in 1904, when Dublin was still in some ways a more British city than it was to become, not yet as Gaelicized in aspiration and orientation as it would be after 1922 when it became the capital of a Gaelic-identified state. "The Dead" takes place in the earliest phase of the merging of the culture of rural Ireland with that of the urban Catholic middle classes, which later set the tone of city and state, and pushed an older, more Anglo-identified Dublin (that of Bram Stoker or George Bernard Shaw) to the wealthy or bohemian margins. "The Dead" registers an early presence of the dying Irish language as a provocative presence in the mind of English-speaking Ireland, and the beginnings of its long afterlife as a dream within it. After Miss Ivors's challenge, from now on, whether he likes it or not, whether he ever learns it or not, there will always be a suspicion, an accusation, an uncomfortable feeling in Gabriel's mind that English is not truly native to his soul, and that Irish could or should or might have been "his" language. Joyce's depiction of Molly Ivors's challenge to Gabriel is an early intimation in English-speaking Ireland that the Gaelic ideal of the West is where their own true spirit resides, and of the idea, which will become so central to the culture, identity, and dreams of independent Ireland—whether one liked it or not—that even if one spoke only English in one's daily life, even if one did not know Irish at all, one's soul might yet speak Irish.

Irish is referred to but effectively never used in "The Dead." It is a mysterious, unspoken language of a far-off "West," in contrast with the all the chatter and different registers of English used throughout the story. Actual words in Irish have almost no presence in the story except for the (slightly inaccurately used) salutation "Beannacht libh."[4] Gabriel's addled thoughts, which reveal the hidden symbolic depths behind apparently concrete things, present the revivalist vision of Irish as an impossible ideal of a transcendent form of language.

One of the deaths referred to in the title of Joyce's story, then, is that of Irish, the death being witnessed, if mutely, at that very historical moment in Tumgesh and Carrowliam Beg, but one that seems far removed from Usher's Island and from the Dublin of the Conroys and the Misses Morkan. Miss Ivors does evoke a place on the other side of Ireland—the Aran Islands—where Gaelic is still alive, but in "The Dead" the West is an idea more than a place, standing, almost by definition, for a distant, mythical location, for somewhere emblematically removed from the social world of the story.

In actual fact, native Irish was closer in place and time to Edwardian Dublin than Gabriel seems to think. As "Eveline" may subtly suggest, many of the inhabitants of Dublin in 1904 must have had some memories of native spoken Irish, such as those who had moved to Dublin from other parts of Ireland where the language was or had been spoken, or whose parents or grandparents or servants had done so. Through Nora, Joyce himself was only one degree of separation from Irish-speaking Ireland: her home district of Bowling Green was still substantially Irish-speaking in the early twentieth century, and the 1901 census records Nora's mother, Annie, as a speaker of Irish and English. As a seamstress born in 1861, Annie could only have acquired this Irish at home, so she was certainly a native speaker of some sort. The Barnacles' return for 1901 replicates the pattern of my great-grandmother's household in Carrowliam Beg, with bilingual parents and monoglot English-speaking children. Nora must have heard plenty of native Irish in her childhood, either at home or in the neighborhood. Most compellingly of all for readers of Joyce, the census returns suggest that Michael Feeney and "Sonny" Bodkin, the two likely models for Gretta's dead admirer, Michael Furey, were probably native speakers of Irish.

Even without this extraneous biographical information, the Irish language can be found woven through the story's many reflections on death. Despite Gretta's fresh, wounded memories of Michael

Furey, he is lost to her, to life, forever. There is an implicit parallel in the story between Gretta's pining for her dead lover, her craving to be in his presence once again, and Miss Ivors (and her fellow Gaelic Leaguers) pining for the lost Irish-speaking world, desiring the language to live again. After all, the West of the story is both a real place where Irish is still the everyday language of the people and a supernatural realm where one can commune with the souls of the deceased, "that region where dwell the vast hosts of the dead."

Individuals are as cut off from one other, the story suggests, as the living are from the dead: Gabriel is as divided from Gretta as much as Gretta is from the deceased Michael Furey. These bleak meditations are woven through with questions of language revivalism: the Gaelic League is a presence in "The Dead" neither because Joyce wished to mock it nor because he thought its prescriptions offered a solution to a nation in search of a destiny, but rather because he sensed that within the passions of Irish language revivalism, in its grieving for a lost, doomed tongue in which it was imagined the soul might have found a true means of expression, there lay hidden dreams and energies that had nothing to do with patriotism or nationalism but with deeper, unspoken longings about language itself, the very same ones that were a major impulse for mainstream European modernism, the sense that all language is foreign, that our souls and minds are always cast adrift in a language that is alien to them.

In 1922, eighteen years after the fictional Christmas party in Usher's Island, the convictions of Molly Ivors and her comrades in the league, new and radical in 1904, were part of the founding official ideologies of the new Irish Free State. In "The Dead," Joyce identifies broader yearnings underpinning the patriotic beliefs and efforts of the Irish language revivalist movement. The often-mocked unrealistic nature of the movement's aspirations—to convert Ireland back to Gaelic in a few generations—is cast in a new light by this connection. These parallels are not drawn explicitly in the story, and the revivalists themselves were not aware of their common feeling with modernist poets and writers who dreamed of finding new languages for art and experience.

The Dream of Irish

"The Dead" registers the presence of the language at a particular transitional moment, the birth of the dream of national Irish out of the death of vernacular Irish. From this moment on, Irish began to cleave between native Irish (the everyday language of the longed-for West) and revivalist Irish (the greeting *beannacht libh* used at a Dublin party as a political gesture). These intense symbolic meanings accrued to Irish only late in its life, and they have to do with the highly unusual way in which the distinction between native and nonnative speakers of the language arose and developed over the twentieth century.

Since its demise as a widely spoken tongue, Irish has been the object of perhaps the most sustained and elaborate series of imaginative and symbolic investments of any endangered language. Its restoration and revival were the first national aim of the new Irish government in 1922; it was actively backed by a state and named in the 1937 constitution as the "first official language"; compulsory in primary and secondary schools, for some state jobs, and for entry to the National University; an ideology so central to national life that it provoked the formation of groups (notably the Language Freedom Movement) opposed to its official promotion.

It bears repeating that the instrumental role the language movement played in the political struggles that led to the foundation of the Irish state was a new and thoroughly modern phenomenon (perhaps still a unique one). The coupling of the ideal of national independence with a language, as Benedict Anderson points out in a different context, was far from a given; still less so, one might suppose, when the language in question was known by a small minority of the nation's citizens (a minority often unconcerned with maintaining it). In the early nineteenth century, the anti-imperialist Irish political leader Daniel O'Connell encouraged people to switch to English as a more effective vehicle for the struggle for national emancipation. O'Connell, himself a native Irish speaker, was still addressing a country where Irish was widespread as the ordinary language of rural people (even still in parts of the east) and not yet loaded with the weight of bigger ideas, not yet charged with being a language of the soul. A century later, when the language was on the verge of disappearing as a natural vernacular, the idea of an Irish patriot who did not support the language revival movement was all but unthinkable.

Despite the great disappointments the language movement has suffered, it would be a mistake to view the outcome of the national aim of restoring the Irish language as a failure. More is written and printed in Irish now than at any other time in its history; it has a dedicated and high-quality television station; it retains a central place in the education system; it has a still notable symbolic role in Irish public life and it commands widespread goodwill (increasingly so, by some measures). More people declare themselves able to speak Irish than ever before, even if the levels of actual competence are dubious. But in other respects, the ways in which Irish is felt to be dead or dying in "The Dead" became more acutely true as the twentieth century wore on. As a spontaneous vernacular, a medium of family or community life, a language of intimacy and everyday interactions, Irish has become rarer and rarer, now restricted to a few isolated patches, and even there showing signs of dwindling.[5] Native spoken Irish is something that one needs to go looking for; it is a rare thing indeed to encounter it by accident. In 1904, Miss Ivors and her friends could have come across pockets of native Irish even before they crossed the Shannon;[6] in the twenty-first century, they would have to push all the way to the coast and then farther west again before hearing it. Irish today is often found in dedicated, frequently state-sponsored, environments but only rarely found in nature, as it were.

The question of whether the language is dead or alive—even if such a simple binary is inadequate to describe its situation—is, and has long been, central to discourse about the language. The term has become such a loaded one that the title of Reg Hindley's sympathetic and scrupulous study of language shift in Irish-speaking areas, *The Death of the Irish Language*, was considered by many language enthusiasts to be an unacceptable provocation. Those who oppose the language's continued role in education and government describe Irish as dead, and its proponents' key claim is that it is a "living language."

Nuala Ní Dhomhnaill's 1995 essay on her decision to write in Irish is entitled "Why I Choose to Write in Irish, the Corpse That Sits Up and Talks Back."[7] So whether one believes that Irish is dead or alive, or whether one wishes it were one or the other, in the twentieth century (and in the twenty-first) the idea of Irish is inescapably bound up with the idea of language death. The terms of life and death, of survival, revival, renaissance, terminal decline, and so on, as Joyce's story subtly registers early on, are part of what the language has come to mean. Optimistic declarations and exaggerations about the extent to which Irish is spoken, and talking up the statistics, are almost considered requirements to show support for the language, a convention which suggests that modern Irish is a dream as well as a language, and that it is this dream, whatever it may be, that excites the energies of many of its advocates.

More—far more—has been written in or about Irish since the mid-twentieth century, the period when its number of native speakers has never been lower, than at any other time in its long history. The energies that have been devoted to Irish during this period are usually casually attributed to a wider discourse of nationalism, patriotism, or nostalgia. But when viewed in a comparative European context, these explanations quickly prove inadequate. Ever since it could no longer be taken for granted as a generally used language of everyday life, Irish has had a dramatic second life, or, we might say, afterlife, as a linguistic ideal, the focus of an enormous amount of projections, hopes, fears, and disappointments; the object of mysterious yearnings and the carrier of obscure dreams which have dressed themselves in the guise of politics and nationalism but which are really part of a wider set of responses to the cultural challenges of modernity.

While much of this book is concerned with exploring the parallels in how language change affected modernist literature in Ireland, France, and Italy, it is important to remember that the history of Irish—one of the oldest vernacular literatures in Europe—is also highly exceptional. For about one thousand five hundred years Irish was the only language, or close to it, spoken by the population of the island. From the tenth century, the Vikings established some small

Norse-speaking ports, and from the twelfth century onward, a significant Norman-French population was added to the population. But both Norse and Norman French, and later the Middle English that spread from Dublin, were mostly linguistically assimilated to Irish over time, and Irish remained the principal language of both everyday life and high culture on the island. Only the deliberate settlement of large tracts of the country with British colonists in the sixteenth and seventeenth centuries and the defeat of the native aristocracy, for whom literary patronage had been a key part of their social function, began to seriously undermine the status of the language. Its life as a high poetic language—employing a literary standard and set of complex meters that were shared from Kerry to the Hebrides—came to an abrupt end in the century that followed the battle of Kinsale in 1601 when the Gaelic aristocracy was defeated and its leaders fled to the Continent. Thereafter, Irish became not only the language of a dispossessed people but the very badge of dispossession, poverty, and backwardness. It retreated to oral and local use; English became the language of writing and of social advancement. By the middle of the nineteenth century, by some estimations, there were as few as twenty people who were literate in Irish, though this is a highly disputed figure.[8]

Much has been written about the indignity of this demise and its consequences, and even more has been written about the renewal of respect and interest in the language from the late nineteenth century on. But, as my own family history starkly shows, much less is known about the language's spoken history, from being the sole medium of daily life for most of the native population in the seventeenth century to that of disconnected and largely bilingual minorities by the end of the nineteenth. In its existence as a daily spoken language, Irish had a much more lingering decline than it did as a literary medium, an imbalance that was in some ways to reverse itself with the rise of official Irish in the English-speaking Ireland of the twentieth century. During the eighteenth century, spoken Irish experienced a steady erosion that spread westward from the east coast, but outside the towns this change was slow, and in many parts of the island insignificant. Recent

studies have shown that native spoken Irish was far more geographically widespread at the dawn of the nineteenth century than has been
generally assumed (urban merchant families in Dublin and other cities were still using Irish among themselves at the beginning of the
nineteenth century, there were native Irish-speaking communities in
Glenasmole on the outskirts of Dublin as late as the 1830s, and, in
the same decade, the Irish Missionary Society launched a campaign
to distribute Irish-language Bibles to proselytize the peasants of now
thoroughly Anglophone County Meath).[9]

The early decades of the nineteenth century saw a quicker transition to English, a process that gathered dramatic momentum in
the middle of the century. The period from about 1830 to 1870 saw
a decisive and deliberate switch from Irish to English as the vernacular of rural communities throughout most of the island, and
English was starting to take the place of Irish even in remote places
like Tumgesh.[10] By the time Ireland gained its independence in 1922,
around 10 percent of the population spoke Irish, most of whom were
native speakers. A patchy sort of bilingualism had obtained across
much of the island through the eighteenth century. But as Irish ceased
to be spoken throughout large areas of the country, those districts
that through isolation, poverty, or lack of education had remained
Irish-speaking began to take on a collective, exceptional identity in
the mind of the country and became known, by analogy with a Scottish term, as the "Gaeltacht" (as opposed to the "Galltacht," made up
of English-speaking areas).[11] "The Dead" plays on the new awareness at the beginning of the century of the Gaeltacht as a distinct
cultural zone within Ireland. In 1926, the government of the newly
independent Irish Free State, showing just how pervasive the influence of the language movement had been on the political struggle,
declared its first national aim to be that of preserving and restoring
the Irish language (as we shall see, these are in fact two quite different aims). To implement the first part of this project, preservation,
the government set about institutionalizing these linguistic boundaries and created a commission to "inquire and report . . . as to the
percentage of Irish Speakers in a district which would warrant its

being regarded as (a) an Irish speaking district or (b) a partly Irish speaking district, and the present extent and location of such districts."[12] Liam Cosgrave, the prime minister, wrote at the time he set up the Commission: "The future of the Irish language and its part in the future of the nation depend, more than anything else, on its continuing in an unbroken tradition as the language of Irish homes. This tradition is the living root from which alone organic growth is possible. For this reason, the Irish people rightly value as a national asset their 'Gaeltacht,' the scattered range of districts in which Irish is the home language."[13]

Taking the 1911 census returns as a rough guide to districts where native Irish might have survived, the Gaeltacht Commission sent Gardaí (policemen) to investigate the extent of Irish in their localities. The terms of the commission to establish the boundaries of the Gaeltacht had been drawn up with regard both to description and aspiration.[14] Two categories of Irish-speaking districts were to be distinguished, *fíorGhaeltacht*, "true Gaeltacht" where Irish was the ordinary daily language of the community, like Molly Ivors's Aran, and *breacGhaeltacht*, "speckled Gaeltacht," places where English was used by many, or most, but where Irish was still the mother tongue of more than 25 percent of the population, though of less than 80 percent. Molly Ivors's Aran would have been at the very upper end of the *fíorGhaeltacht*, while Tumgesh was on the very lowest edge of the *breacGhaeltacht* (Tumgesh, in fact, was declassified when the boundaries were later redrawn).[15]

The country was thus officially divided into two official language areas, and native, vernacular Irish officially connected with certain delimited districts. At the same time, government policies emphasized that the Irish people as a whole had lost Irish, and that the language was the birthright of them all. Part of the idea of designating special Gaeltacht areas was also that they were to provide a model and resource for the rest of the country on its supposed patriotic path back to the future from English to Irish.[16] In the 1960s and 1970s this model was to be challenged by some Gaeltacht communities who saw themselves as a linguistic minority within an English-speaking country. Their movement, Gluaiseacht Chearta Siabhialta na Gael-tachta, the Gaeltacht Civil Rights Movement, led to the establishment of the state-funded Irish-language community radio station, Raidió na Gaeltachta, founded in 1972.

At the time the boundaries were established, native speakers constituted a good majority of Irish speakers. But high levels of emigration from rural areas and the uninterrupted switch from Irish to English within much of the Gaeltacht itself resulted in a steady fall in the number of native speakers. As the compulsory teaching of Irish in the rest of the country was consolidated, the schools produced a whole generation who had been taught Irish as a second language. This educational program had varying degrees of success, but it was enough that within a few decades native speakers were a small and quickly declining proportion of even fluent Irish speakers as a whole, dwarfed in numbers by those that had come to Irish as a second language.

From the first, the Gaelic League had been conflicted about how best to strike a balance between conserving the language in those areas where it was still a living tongue—and whose impoverished speakers were often indifferent or even hostile to their own language—and promoting the study and use of Irish among educated English speakers in the rest of Ireland. Many were uneasy with the consequences for the language itself of producing ever greater numbers of second-language speakers of Irish while the number of native speakers continued inexorably to wane. In a lecture given in 1903, entitled "The Irish Speaking Districts," Patrick Dineen, author of the famous Irish-English dictionary, complained about the league's emphasis on teaching Irish outside the Gaeltacht, at the expense of ensuring its survival in those places where it was still the vernacular of the people:

> The wide extension of the League has a tendency to place the mere student, the mere stammerer in Irish—on terms of equality with the native speaker—nay, to give him the preference. The student of Irish—the stammerer in Irish, if I may so call him without the slightest depreciation—should get every encouragement in our power, but

multiply him a million-fold, and that million of stammering students will be powerless to save from extinction the genuine accents, the native idiom of our vernacular speech. It is the genuine native speaker alone that can hand on the living torch to future generations. It is in the native speaker as a single individual and in groups and combinations that the only hope of the language rests.[17]

Dineen's view was more widely shared at the turn of the century, when native speakers were still relatively thick on the ground if you knew where to look. Twenty years later, while the preservation of the Gaeltacht remained a cornerstone of government language policy, this goal of language preservation was overshadowed by the project of language revival and restoration in the state as a whole. This was partly because teaching Irish in schools, promoting it in the state bureaucracy, and organizing groups and activities for middle-class dreamers and hobbyists proved easier than maintaining the fragile linguistic ecology of remote and poverty-stricken rural communities, and it was easier to produce tangible results in this realm. But it was also a natural consequence of the language ideology of the independent state.[18] For the earliest Anglo-Irish revivalists, whose families had never spoken Irish themselves but whose peasant tenants did, the distinction between native and second-language speakers had been a clear-cut one: William Butler Yeats needed only to walk through the Sligo countryside to hear it spoken. Irish was not exactly a foreign language to Yeats, Augusta Gregory, or John Millington Synge, but it had never been spoken within their own family circles or class, and so they had a clear sense of Irish speakers as a separate community.[19]

But as the use of Irish as a rural vernacular declined, and a coherent community of naturally Irish-speaking individuals became harder to define, the relationship between native and deliberately acquired Irish became a more problematic one. Part of the aim of political and cultural independence was, in Douglas Hyde's famous phrase, the "de-Anglicization of Ireland," that is, the reversal of historical outcomes; distinguishing among different types of Irish, and among different ways of coming to Irish, became a more delicate and fraught issue, since, unlike most of the Anglo-Irish ascendancy,

Irish Catholics could imagine that, had Irish history turned out differently, they might have been Irish speakers from birth.[20] Since Irish was viewed as the birthright of all the Irish people, and its restoration as the predominant spoken language of the whole nation the goal of the movement, placing too much emphasis on the issue of native versus learned Irish risked drawing invidious distinctions within the language movement; worse, it risked treating Irish as a regional language within Ireland—the autochthonous language of the Gaeltacht "reservations" but "foreign" to the Galltacht (similar thinking had been behind the insistence on the term "Irish" rather than "Gaelic" for the language).

The tension between language preservation and language revival has had complex literary ramifications. The literary end of the Irish language revival had found itself hampered from the beginning by the lack of a high written register. Unlike Wales and Scotland, whose Celtic languages were spoken by Bible-reading Protestant populations and maintained a literary standard even as their vernacular use diminished, in Catholic Ireland, the illiteracy of the Irish-speaking population, the absence of a vernacular liturgy, the collapse of the native patronage system, and the geographical fragmentation of the Irish-speaking zone had resulted in the loss of a coherent audience and shared literary standard.[21] It was not clear for those seeking to reestablish a national literature in Irish at the end of the nineteenth century and the beginning of the twentieth where they ought, linguistically, to begin: what kind of Irish one ought to write in to express contemporary ideas and feelings, or to address a national, as opposed to local, audience. The closest thing to a living "high" native tradition was in the somewhat ragged literary conventions of the late eighteenth century, which a number of poets tried unsuccessfully to adapt for twentieth-century purposes.[22] After some attempts at this, and at creating a new standard based on the early modern Irish of Geoffrey Keating, the upper hand in the first decades of the twentieth century was gained by a movement dedicated to *caint na ndaoine*, "the speech of the people." These writers, spearheaded by

Peadar Ua Laoghaire, proposed using the Irish spoken by the people of the Gaeltacht as the basis for the literary language.

The problems with this were numerous, and they came to a head in the decades we are concerned with here, the 1940s and 1950s. Using *caint na ndaoine* as a model meant, first of all, that all writing in Irish was by necessity not merely regionally inflected but, since the districts where Irish was still spoken were so few and far between, it was tied to highly specific localities, even to individual hamlets, valleys, or islands. Second of all, the "people" referred to in "the speech of the people" were small populations who lived traditional rural lives of fishing, small farming, and, it must be said, of great want and hardship. They had access in many instances to an impressive and sophisticated oral literature, and there were some successful prose works about Gaeltacht life produced in *caint na ndaoine*, but how these essentially unwritten and quite divergent idioms could be harnessed for the purposes of creating a unified national literature capable of expressing a contemporary sensibility was unclear. In the first phase of the revival, when there was still a substantial pool of native speakers, and sizable stretches of territory where Irish was usual language, the idea of a standard based on spoken Gaeltacht Irish was already a problematic proposition; by the 1940s, when the number of native speakers had greatly diminished, and vernacular Irish was confined to but a handful of places, it began to seem untenable.

Moreover, the artistic goals that had been so central to the first decades of the Gaelic League, and to academic activists such as Gregory, Patrick Pearse, and Hyde had been largely sidelined or forgotten by the 1940s. Before independence, the language movement had been of a piece with the ideals of the English-language Irish literary revival of the same years, and it counted plenty of Protestants among its leaders. But in the decades following the foundation of the state, the project of reviving the Irish language took on a very different, aggressively Catholic complexion. The poetic dreams of the early revivalists were cast aside; the goal in some powerful quarters within the language movement and its now official apparatus was no longer to cultivate the endangered spoken tongue of the western peasantry or to resurrect the old rural Gaelic mindset but to build a new, modern, Catholic, Irish-speaking state. Individual creative endeavor took, at best, second place to this technocratic project of state building. One commentator, Liam Ó Laoghaire, complained in 1940: "We have failed miserably to give our unique language and literature any place in our national life. From the start it was departmentalized as thought itself has been. In the Church, Theatre, Cinema, Sportsground, Factory and Home, what is it worth? It has lent itself to individual exploration perhaps, but to the Nation it has been a charming, if at times troublesome curiosity."[23] A return to the lost Gaelic past—Hyde's cultural "de-Anglicization"—was sidelined in favor of transforming Irish into a language fit for contemporary national needs. Standardizing the written language became a priority, and the older ideal of a literary model based on the speech of rural native speakers was at odds with the statist modernizing zeal. The idea of the poet, so central in the revival—Irish-language and Anglophone alike—of Joyce's time was now much more peripheral. Indeed, An Gúm, the government agency responsible for commissioning and publishing books in Irish had an explicit policy of discouraging original work in favor of translations, mostly from English; many of the most talented Irish-language writers of the time earned their living from the surreal task of producing Irish-language versions of Shakespeare, Dickens, and even Joyce.[24]

The intensity of the debates in mid-twentieth-century Ireland surrounding the official aim of restoring Irish—when the rest of western Europe was fighting and then dealing with the aftermath of the Second World War—is hard to understand nowadays, when the Irish language is a far less contentious field, less full of utopian promise for its champions and less threatening for its detractors. But in the 1930s, 40s, and 50s, the language question was a live and controversial one.[25] The idea still persisted that a mass restoration of the language might yet be possible, a hope for some, a fear for others. There was a sense on all sides, supporters and enemies, that the language movement encompassed and affected everyone in the state.

Some responded to "the language question" by devoting efforts to acquiring and mastering the language as a literary medium for themselves; others feared and despised the hypocrisy of the language revival movement and feared it was a costly and regressive obstacle to economic and social progress, to national cohesion or even to national unification. The Language Freedom Movement, founded in 1966—and supported by the native Irish-speaking novelist Séamus Ó Grianna—to oppose compulsory Irish in the education system and state bureaucracy—was feeding off energies that had been bubbling throughout the previous decades. For both groups, revivalists and antirevivalists, Irish was in some way or another a looming presence that needed to be dealt with.

The 1940s and 1950s in the rest of western Europe set an agenda that was to utterly transform society and culture. In many places—France, Italy, northern Germany—this included the accelerated decline and occasionally loss of local dialects and small languages. In Ireland, even though the decline of Irish had irrevocably already taken place, modern notions of what the Irish language is were also set and crystallized in those decades. For one thing, the balance between preservation and revival was definitively settled in favor of the latter, with the contraction and depopulation of the Gaeltacht accompanying the ongoing mass production of second-language speakers and the promotion of official, state-sponsored Irish in a variety of domains. Patterns of use for the Irish language outside the Gaeltacht were established, extended and normalized, while the Gaeltacht itself remained blighted by poverty and emigration.

Why Write in Irish?

Although the use of Irish in the Gaeltacht, unlike in the rest of the country, was not extended during the 1940s and 1950s, the geographical areas in which Irish was normally spoken—which had been in constant shrinkage since the sixteenth century—finally stabilized during these decades and did not shift again until the 1980s and 1990s. Native Irish has continued to this day as a community language in three core areas within the official Gaeltacht, conforming to a geographical pattern set in the 1950s: south-central Connemara and its offshore islands (including Aran), the largest and most vibrant surviving Irish-speaking area; a part of northwest Donegal; and the smallest and most embattled Irish-speaking area, but the one most important for Irish-language poetry in the twentieth century (and before), the last stronghold of Munster Irish in the area known as Corca Dhuibhne, most famously in and around the parish of Dún Chaoin, on the far western tip of the Dingle Peninsula in County Kerry. In these areas literary production by the diminishing pool of native speakers never ceased.

We can identify four main strains of native writing in Irish in the twentieth century, two of which faded in the 1940s but whose effects and influence are still felt, and two of which have continued to the present day. The first came in the sudden flurry of autobiographies produced by talented storytellers from the Blasket Islands in west Kerry in the 1920s, cultivated and promoted by English and Scandinavian anthropologists.[26] These reached international fame in translation (E. M. Forster wrote the introduction to the English translation of Tomás Criomhthain's *An tOileánach* (*The Islandman*) (1929; English translation 1934). They had an enormous psychological effect on twentieth-century Irish-language writing as a whole, their linguistic richness an object of emulation and envy for other Irish-language writers, their relentless detailing of peasant poverty and tragedy one of satire and ridicule for others, notably in Flann O'Brien's comic masterpiece *An Béal Bocht* (*The Poor Mouth*) (1941).[27] A second category can be discerned in the Gaeltacht realism pioneered by Peadar Ua Laoghaire, including novels and short stories by writers such as Pádraic Ó Conaire (though not a native speaker himself), Micí Mac Gabhann, and Liam O'Flaherty (the last of whom wrote only occasionally in his native Irish). In the second half of the century, two more genres of literary production by native speakers persisted. As Gearóid Denvir points out, the long and much vaunted tradition of oral poetic composition did not come to an end, as is usually claimed, with the death of Raftery, the last of the bards, in

1835.[28] The matter of the great bards, as Denvir says, had always been local; as the physical territory in which Irish was spoken shrank, this poetic activity did not cease but simply became restricted to smaller and smaller enclaves, where popular, locally oriented poetic and song composition still exists to this day[29] (for Raftery it was Ireland west of the Shannon; for the contemporary Connemara poet, Joe Steve Ó Neachtain, it is the Cois Fhairrge district of south Galway).[30] We may count this as the third category of modern literary production by native speakers. Fourth, and perhaps most important for our purposes, there have been a small but significant number of individual native-speaking writers who pioneered modernist literary techniques. Chief among these were Máirtín Ó Direáin, a poet from the Aran Islands, and the Connemara novelist Máirtín Ó Cadhain, whose *Cré na Cille* ("Churchyard Clay") (1949) is considered to be an unrivaled achievement of modern Irish fiction.[31]

To focus on the use of Irish as a second language is not to dismiss the importance and complexity of this body of work, which continues to this day, but rather to respect its particularity. Native command of Irish is the exception rather than the rule in the spoken language, and this is even more acutely the case in written Irish. While the day-to-day language of almost the whole country (other than the three districts mentioned above, along with a few other smaller pockets) is English, what we might call the psychological linguistic reality is one in which, even if it is rarely concretely used, Irish lurks in the imaginations and memories, to one extent or another, in positive, negative, and neutral ways, conscious or unconscious or semiconscious, of most of the population, whether they speak Irish or not, whether they speak it well or badly. To confuse the way Irish is still used spontaneously in the few places where it has an unbroken tradition as a living language with its wistful, troubling presence in the rest of Ireland is to miss the importance and meaning of what Irish became after it had died out in places like Tumgesh but had taken on a new, placeless afterlife in the national psyche.

This literary production by writers for whom Irish was their mother tongue is totally eclipsed by the amount of literature published in

Irish in the twentieth century by writers who were brought up in English and who chose to write in Irish even though it was their second language, usually acquired at school. The particularity of their self-imposed predicament, and the broader desires their project represents, are hidden if we group them and their output along with bona fide Gaeltacht writers into a single category of "Irish speakers."

The comparative dearth of prose fiction in modern Irish—a pattern that seems to be largely replicated in other minor languages—can be linked to the kinds of imaginative possibilities unleashed by the embattled situation of the language.[32] In his last essay, "Páipéir Bhána agus Páipéir Bhreaca" ("White Papers and Speckled Papers"), Ó Cadhain bitterly criticized the dominance of poetry in Irish-language literature:

> It is a threatening and ominous portent when there is an excessive zeal to compose poetry rather than prose. This is also the situation in other minority languages, including Scots Gaelic. . . . As far as I can make out, far more poetry is being written in Irish than in English here in Ireland. . . . Prose is the concrete base, the mason's cornerstone of life; and it is as rough and unpleasant as life itself. [Translation by Declan Kiberd]
>
> [Staid bhagarach, drochthuar é, an iomarca tóir a bheith ar fhilíocht a chuma le hais an phróis. Seo mar tá sé i mionteangachaí eile ar nós Gàidhlig na hAlban . . . Chó fada is is léar dhomsa is mó go bhfuil d'fhilíocht agus dhá scríobh sa nGaeilge ná sa mBéarla in Éirinn. . . . Sé an prós tathán coincréad, clocha saorsinne an tsaoil, agus é chó garbh, míthaitneamhach leis an saol féin.][33]

Ó Cadhain himself wrote *Cré na Cille*, the only widely acknowledged masterpiece of modernist Irish-language prose. But Ó Cadhain is truly an exception that proves a rule: having grown up in the heart of the living Connemara Gaeltacht, he was also one of the few twentieth-century writers for whom Irish could still be felt as the "concrete base" of life. More telling than the relative preponderance of poetry over prose in modernist Irish-language literature is that fact that the small corpus of significant prose works produced in Irish have tended, unlike the far larger body of poetry, to be written by native speakers from the Gaeltacht. Novels and short stories, rooted as they are in events and in social interactions, are inescapably bound to the vernacular.[34] A contract of realism with the reader requires a novel to be set in a plausible linguistic community. More force again is given to this idea by the fact that both of the most successful literary novelists in Irish, Ó Cadhain and Seosamh Mac Grianna, were not only native speakers but came from south Connemara and northwest Donegal, respectively, places whose dialects have been far less prestigious for poetry but which constitute the two most extensive continuous geographical blocs of Irish-speaking territory.[35] As these areas and their populations have diminished in size, the possibilities for realist fiction in Irish have been severely reduced.[36]

Realist prose is inseparable from bodies and physical territory, and so its production in Irish has declined along with the Gaeltacht. For a modern poet, on the other hand, the gradual unmooring of the language from daily life, from mouths and geographical places, may offer distinct lyrical possibilities. Since the pursuit of the communal cultural ideal of Irish involves, for the individual poet, inhabiting a poetic realm that is exiled from the warmth and rough-and-tumble of quotidian living, from the language of emotional relationships and of childhood memories, we might think of the choice to abandon English for Irish as a modernist form of what in early Christian Ireland was known as "white martyrdom," going into exile from one's homeland and community.

The active literary readership of Irish language poetry is numbered in the low hundreds. By forsaking English for Irish, poets are deliberately reducing their audience to an infinitesimal fragment of what it might be if they wrote in English, their first language. Few native speakers have the time or inclination to read difficult modern poetry in Irish, and in any case, the kind of Irish in which this poetry is written is often not familiar to them.[37] The fact is that the audience is in some respects not merely small, it is nonexistent; modern poetry in Irish is, like *Finnegans Wake* or "The Waste Land," addressed to an ideal hypothesis of a reader that cannot exist in the real world.

The 1940s and 1950s simultaneously witnessed the sudden emergence of modern poetry in Irish and the final, definitive retreat of the native language into a handful of small enclaves.[38] For all the stifling conservatism of the state-backed movement to revive the Irish language in the 1930s, 40s, and 50s, and for all its apparently frustrating lack of realism, this very cult of unreality, of disappointment and failure mixed with utopian energies, may have fed, more than hindered, this poetic event.

Deciding to write in Irish has been viewed since the time of the Gaelic League as a political, patriotic decision, even sacrifice, the fulfillment of an obvious obligation—or perceived obligation—to the nation, rather than as a matter of literary preference. This was the view expressed by Daniel Corkery in *The Fortunes of the Irish Language:* "The tradition of the Irish people is to be understood and experienced with intimacy only in the Irish tongue," or by Yeats who wrote in a letter to the *Leader* in 1900 that "the mass of people in this country cease to understand any poetry when they cease to understand [Irish]."[39] This theory of national poetry suggests that the Irish people as a collective are native Irish speakers, even if as individuals their native language is largely English, and that the withering away of the native language is the enemy of the Irish-language poet.

But we might more profitably read the losses, difficulties, and strivings implicit in their abandonment of English and the hopes of a new "home" in Irish as constituting in some cases a poetic impulse of its own, one built upon the idea of homelessness and nurtured rather than hindered by the troubles and difficulties in which Irish found itself by the mid-twentieth century.

two

THE QUEER LINGUISTIC UTOPIA OF
PIER PAOLO PASOLINI

The 1940s and 1950s, the decades that set the patterns of use and meaning for modern Irish, were also a turning point in the linguistic history of Italy. If Irish was definitively divided into two Irishes, native and "national," in the period, these years also saw a new consciousness in Italy about what using dialect instead of standard Italian could mean, and especially, about the possibilities of deliberately choosing dialect as a literary medium. There are few meaningful sociolinguistic similarities between Ireland and Italy, but there are striking parallels in how vernacular change caused languages and dialects to become imbued with a special literary significance. Italy provides a more revealing comparative context for Ireland in this regard than anywhere else because it is the only example of a country in Europe where the deliberate adoption of minor speech forms for poetic purposes in the twentieth century has been reflected on and analyzed as a poetic, rather than merely political or local, practice.

In sociolinguistic terms, the closest analogues to modern Irish would be languages like Basque and Welsh, philologically distinct from the major language rival, with a small, shrinking native-speaker base and a substantial life as a second, learned language with an emblematic national role. But despite these similarities in the position of the spoken and the official language, the *literary* significance that Irish acquired in the wake of its vernacular decline finds a richer comparison in the literary use of dialects in twentieth-century Italy. There is no individual dialect within Italy that lends itself to direct historical or sociological comparison with Irish; what is of interest to us here is the discovery in the twentieth century of the literary possibilities of dialect per se, as an alternative form of poetic language that offered an antidote to the feeling that language itself had become commodified and evacuated of life.

The parallels between modern literature in Irish and in Italian dialects are all the more striking because of the sociohistorical differences between the two situations: they resemble each other only in this peculiar literary respect, as utopian literary dreams of an alternative form of language. In every other respect, the linguistic situations are different. To begin with, although the Irish language movement and the neodialect tradition in Italy are connected to a vernacular decline, the timing, the extent, and the mode of decline have little in common in the two cases. The widespread use of standard Italian instead of dialect as a daily language in Italy really dates only from the aftermath of the Second World War, more than a century after English had definitively overtaken Irish in Ireland.[1] Second, the nature of how the linguistic change occurred is hardly comparable. All of the varieties covered by the umbrella term *dialetto* are, by definition, autochthonous to the Italian national territory, whereas English was brought to Ireland by a foreign colonizing power, and the cultural infrastructure of Irish was deliberately, indeed violently, dismantled. The adoption of English as the daily speech of the countryside was hastened by starvation and social collapse. In Italy, although poverty and emigration both played a role in the spread of spoken standard Italian at the expense of dialect, and although the collapse in peasant culture that accompanied the vernacular shift was sudden and traumatic, the major drivers of linguistic change were the "softer" postwar agents of radio, newspapers, internal migration, mass primary education, and compulsory military service.[2]

Nor are the differences limited to these historical, sociolinguistic questions of how, when, and to what degree vernacular change occurred. Perhaps even more significant for our purposes is the philological issue of the genetic linguistic relationships: Irish and English are wholly foreign languages, barely related to one another at all, whereas all of the Italian dialects, including the standard, are close relatives. Italian and the dialects are derived from a common ancestor: the official Tuscan-based standard is only one of several descendants of Latin but was consciously promoted as a pan-regional national tongue. Many of the dialects are to some degree mutually intelligible (although this varies widely), and Italian and dialects all share at the very least a basic Romance lexical and grammatical framework. This means that it is an easy enough matter, with exposure, to acquire at least a passive knowledge of the standard (or of a given dialect), and that code-switching and diglossia, in which the standard feels like the formal or written version of one's dialect, rather than a wholly foreign imposition, are common. It also means that most dialects can be spoken in mixed versions, across a continuum from pure dialect to pure standard, with any number of hybrid forms in between. This is obviously an impossibility to imagine with Irish and English, whose family connection is lost in the most distant Indo-European mists of time. The close philological relationship of the Italian dialects to one another meant that Italy was never plunged into the traumatic linguistic chaos that characterized much of Ireland in the nineteenth century.

Yet the long and complex tradition of thought in Italy on the relationship between these two registers, long available to educated Italians, furnishes telling insights on the uses and meanings of modern Irish. The comparative ease with which speakers can learn or move between dialect and standard Italian, the length and relative peace of the cohabitation on the peninsula between local spoken idioms and a shared formal and written standard, and, most of all, the different role of language questions in national politics, have allowed metalinguistic reflection to be bolder and less ideologically charged than in Ireland, less subject to semicompulsory pieties or simplistic analogies.

The Italian dialects do not correspond to a straightforward concept of a "linguistic minority." The Italian state does contain minorities of this sort, independent and sometimes embattled linguistic communities whose high or literary language—Greek, Catalan, French, High German—comes or came from a linguistic system outside Italy. These include the Provençal-speaking valleys in western Piedmont, the dialects of German spoken in South Tyrolia, Catalan speakers of Alghero, the Greek- and Albanian-speaking villages of the south, the Slovenes on the borders of the northeast, the French speakers of the Aosta valley, and so on, often the result of shifting political borders or old migrations. What we are concerned with instead are those local forms of speech, native to Italian villages, valleys, and cities, whose speakers consider Italian as their own official or literary standard, the home-grown Italian varieties of Romance, known collectively as "dialect," or in Italian, *dialetto*.

Dialetto is a generic term that refers to all local forms of Romance speech indigenous to Italy, defined in opposition to *lingua*, the standard literary Italian language, based on Tuscan and designed for use throughout the nation. It is important to stress that the binary between *dialetto* and *lingua* is not a philological distinction but refers to different social functions of language, corresponding to what the Prague school of linguistics distinguishes as "folk speech" and "standard speech." Italian dialects are not descendants of or deformations of standard Italian but idioms that are used for local and casual rather than interregional or formal purposes. Some "dialects," such as Roman or Umbrian, are closely related to Tuscan and easily intelligible to someone who speaks the national language, whereas others are more distant. Some would ordinarily be considered different languages, such as Sardinian, a Romance family in its own right, or—the example that we shall be looking at here—Friulian, which some (though by no means all) linguists consider to be part of the Raetian rather than Italic subgroup of Romance languages.[3]

The origins of the Italian dialects, as in France and elsewhere in the Romance-speaking world, are to be found in the disintegration from about A.D. 400 onward of the sophisticated communications network of the Roman Empire. With the degradation of the old Roman roads and transport systems, distances became greater, life became more local, and the spoken language of the Romanized world—which had always differed from formal written Latin—split into multiple local varieties. As was to be the case with standard Italian almost two thousand years later, the maintenance of a uniform Latin standard had depended on literacy; as the Roman education system collapsed, literacy declined with it.[4] The combination of these things—drastically reduced mobility, lack of formal education, illiteracy—meant that social, commercial, and cultural life became more and more confined to the immediate locality. With ever less contact among speakers of distant forms of "Latin," the spoken forms of the language became molded by small communities, and Latin fragmented into a mosaic of thousands of local vernaculars, dialects wholly identifiable with specific places, forms of language whose boundaries were set by the natural landscape, rivers, valleys, mountains.

The spoken language of Tuscany was but one more of these forms, until the fourteenth century, when it became the basis for a literary model to be emulated for writers from all over Italy. As Tuscan became the "national" language, the other forms of spoken Romance in Italy (a number of which had distinguished literary pasts in their own right) became confined to local use, as a casual medium for conversation at home or in the immediate community, and labeled "dialect" as opposed to the Tuscan *lingua*, "language."

The word *dialetto* thus encompasses hundreds of local idioms, from Trieste to Calabria, each with a distinct history and situation. Some of them, such as Neapolitan or Venetian, had literary traditions of their own, others have been a vehicle mostly for popular songs or comedy, while some were never really written at all. *Dialetto* was traditionally used for colloquial and intimate conversation in the family and local community, with Italian, *lingua*, the national form intended for use across all regions of Italy, associated with formal and written communication. Knowledge of the standard language has long been associated with literacy—Italian was the language one learned to write in; by learning to write one learned Italian. This remained the situation in Italy more or less until the Second World War, after which Italian began to supplant dialect as the medium of daily local life.

Writing in dialect as a self-conscious, deliberate choice only really became possible in the seventeenth century when the hegemony of Tuscan (or, more accurately, a standardized form of fourteenth-century Florentine) as *the* literary language of Italy really established itself and it became the ideal written language of all Italians, no matter where they came from: *lingua toscana in bocca romana*, "Tuscan language in a Roman mouth," as a saying has it. During this time, indeed, there was an outburst of interest in dialects and in writing them.[5] Only from this point on could an Italian writer conceive of his or her own dialect as a local or intimate alternative to a single "standard."[6] While educated Italian writers have been effectively bilingual for centuries, speakers of their home dialect and writers of the standard language, the idea of local dialects as a possible distinct literary register, as a "minor-language" alternative to writing in *lingua* is a different matter altogether.

Before the eighteenth century it was a common practice in Europe to write in a language other than the language one spoke in everyday conversation, and indeed to write in a language that in a vernacular sense was dead. This is true not only of the use of Latin as a language of science and culture but also for the many Europeans who spoke a language or dialect at home—such as Picard or Gascon—and used a formal standard—in these cases, French—for written purposes (an analogous situation holds today in Luxembourg or in German-speaking Switzerland). It would have been the case for many of the inhabitants of the Hapsburg Empire (where Latin was the language of bureaucracy and administration). The awkwardness—but, for the bourgeoisie, social necessity—of adopting standard German as a spoken language instead of *Plattdeutsch*, is a running theme in Thomas Mann's novel *Buddenbrooks*.

It is especially true in the case of Italian literature, whose standard could hardly have been considered a mother tongue for almost any of the writers who used it in different times and places, and whose popular adoption as a spoken language came much later than that of German in Germany. At the moment of Italian unification in 1860, only a minuscule fraction of Italians—the figure usually given is 2.5 percent—were speakers of the standard.[7] Unlike in France, where the standard French of Paris and environs was also the spoken language of many of the bourgeoisie and townspeople all over France, in Italy the literary language remained largely that: a language of writing alone, with little presence in the daily spoken life of most Italians, and one that could in certain respects be considered as far removed from daily life as Latin. In the middle of the nineteenth century, a Turinese noblewoman explained to a curious American traveler that, even for the members of Parliament in the newly unified Italy, Italian was a "dead language" that they were forced to speak:

> Apart from the Savoyards, who sometimes use French, all of the members of [the Italian] parliament . . . speak in Italian; but for them it is a dead language, in which they are not even accustomed to converse.
> [Eccetto i savoiardi, che qualche volta usano il francese, tutti i deputati . . . parlano in italiano; ma questo è per loro una lingua morta, nella quale non sono nemmeno mai stati abituati a conversare.]

This was the case even for Tuscans. In Florence, one Vincenzo Salvagnoli used the same terms in lamenting that Italian differed from French or English, because one could speak those written languages, whereas Italian, even for a Florentine, was a "dead language":

> In French or in English one writes as one speaks. But if I were to speak the language of Machiavelli I would sound ridiculous; if I were to write as I speak it would sound intolerably vulgar. Even for a Tuscan, that is to say, written Italian is a dead language.
> [In francese o in inglese si scrive come si parla. Ma se io dovessi parlare la lingua di Machiavelli sarei ridicolo; se dovessi scrivere come parlo, suonerebbe intollerabilmente volgare. Anche per un toscano, perciò, l'italiano scritto è una lingua morta.][8]

The nineteenth-century poets Carlo Porta and Gioachino Belli introduced, in a sense, the idea of dialect as an alternative literary medium, by producing truly literary compositions in their respective dialects of Milan and Rome (two cities where the role of dialect was quite distinct). Porta and Belli certainly had their attention drawn to the written possibilities of their oral mother tongues by the strains of Romanticism that were drifting south from Germany, and the real philological energy devoted to the study of the dialects of Italy, which took off later in the century, was prompted by an uneasy sense that the dialects might not always be there, and certainly not in their "pure" form. Even if no less a personage than King Victor Emmanuel II did not know enough Italian to speak it with his ministers—Cavour had to translate for him from Piedmontese[9]—it was clear after 1860 that the unification of Italy would bring about a greater degree of linguistic uniformity.

The sense that dialect was a precious resource that might be lost therefore predates by some stretch the actual decline in the spoken use of the dialects themselves.[10] This did not really gather serious pace until the decades following the Second World War. Knowledge and use of Italian had been slowly growing, in tandem with literacy, since Unification. But the social upheavals and technological advances that came in the wake of the Second World War—the rise of mass broadcasting, literacy, internal migration on a vast scale, improvements in transport and communications, and, most of all, the sudden collapse of the age-old peasant way of life—would set in motion a process of more rapid and more profound linguistic change in Italy. In 1951, two-thirds of the population still used dialect *exclusively* in their daily lives, and most of the other third used both dialect and Italian; a mere decade later, fewer than one in ten Italians lived their lives wholly in dialect, and a full third of the population now never used dialect at all.[11] This process was regionally uneven—dialect-speaking being strongest in the northeast and south, and the use of Italian as a vernacular most extensive in the center—but the trend toward using the standard language in the intimate or casual settings once reserved for dialect was notable everywhere in the wake of the war, and accelerated everywhere as the century went on. The nature of the dialects themselves changed in these decades too, becoming more and more infused with Italian vocabulary, grammatical structures, diction, style, and even phonology (a process common to many minor languages that exist in a state of diglossia with a major one).[12]

Dialect took on a whole new possibility of meaning at the moment in the twentieth century when its givenness as the normal form of colloquial speech for Italians began to be cast into doubt. As many of the dialects began suddenly to fall out of everyday spoken use, choosing to write in dialect began to *mean* something in itself. Many scholars of modern Italian poetry have commented on the apparently ironic coincidence between the decline in the ordinary spoken use of the dialects and their sudden flourishing as literary mediums, with rhetoric that offers a striking parallel to the Irish situation. Franco Brevini wrote that in the late twentieth century "the dialect tradition is registering . . . an unforeseen poetic renewal that coincides with the most serious crisis that the dialects have ever experienced at the level of [spoken] usage [la tradizione dialettale registra . . . un'imprevedibile rinnovamento poetico, che cade in coincidenza con la crisi più grave mai vissuta dai dialetti a livello dell'uso]."[13] The parallel with Irish is all the more instructive because the historical process is uneven throughout Italy; like the coexistence in Ireland of communities of native speakers who wished to shed the language for social advancement, and English-speaking Irish revivalists who wished to learn it, "dialect" means different things in different circumstances. As in Ireland, commentators in Italy have believed their own linguistic paradox to be unique:

A strange destiny, that of the dialects in Italy: ignored by official culture when everyone spoke them, reluctantly alluded to in ministerial reports and programs when they were the only tool possessed by the pupils; now that they are living an ever more feeble existence, as an anomaly on the margins of [standard Italian], they have come to know the—almost posthumous—glory of literary fame, academic attention, even a role in schools. . . . We can see the same contradiction if we look around us, in Italy; where dialect has disappeared, laments are raised for the greater expressivity it supposedly offered; in other places it is far too alive, and the laments are for [its] connotations of backwardness.

[Uno strano destino, quello dei dialetti in Italia: ignorati dalla cultura ufficiale quando tutti li parlavano, nominati con riluttanza nelle relazioni e nei programmi ministeriali quando erano l'unico strumento posseduto dagli scolari, ora che vivono una vita sempre più grama, da irregolari, ai margini della lingua, conoscono la gloria, quasi postuma, della celebrazione letteraria, della considerazione scientifica, persino del protagonismo nella scuola. . . . La stessa contraddizione la troviamo guardandoci intorno, in Italia; qua il dialetto è sparito, e si

levano i rimpianti per il più di espressività che sicuramente avrebbe as-
sicurato; là è fin troppo vivo, e si levano i lamenti per le connotazioni
di arretratezza.][14]

But the seeming contradiction here—that the death of the vernacular coincides with a literary rebirth—is from a certain literary point
of view not a contradiction at all. Dialects that fall out of everyday
life and return in literary form are not experiencing life on the one
hand and death on the other but entering a second life, a ghostly, literary afterlife, which can only come about with the reality or at least
imminent prospect of vernacular death.

This is not to say that the turn to dialect in Italy was devoid of
any political dimension. For some writers, Pasolini chief among
them, Italian was tainted by association with Fascism; dialect was
celebrated as an alternative to the language of the regime and its
bureaucracy, and its cultivation was also part of an ideological exaltation of the peasantry and its culture. Even if rural Italy was not
subjugated by colonialism or ravaged by famine, the social changes
that were behind the decline of spoken dialect were extensive.
"Over the course of a few decades," Brevini writes, "an age-old
agricultural-pastoral-artisanal civilization was wiped out [Nel giro di
pochi decenni era stata liquidata una civiltà di tradizione millenaria
come quella agricolo-pastorale e artigianale]."[15] Pasolini himself referred to it as an "anthropological catastrophe."[16]

But if the turn toward dialect by modern Italian writers after the
Second World War, a turn led by Pasolini, was in part a consequence
of the sudden loss of this peasant culture, it was also a new, later
iteration of ideas and anxieties about language that were inherited
from modernism, especially in the form that modernism took on in
the Italy of the Fascist period, in which the ideal of private, invented
languages of art was central to Italian modernist movements such as
hermeticism and futurism, and so on.[17] The extent to which Pasolini
can be considered in the classic sense to be a modernist is not obvious. But the use he makes of dialect, as a formal device in itself, is in
many ways the logical endpoint of the idea, or ideal, of a private lan-

guage or poetic idiolect, which is one of the most distinctive features of modernist poetry, especially in Italy.[18]

As they faded out of daily life, the dialects began to suggest meanings and properties to the literary imagination which they had never had while they were an unremarkable, ubiquitous presence in day-to-day life. Even if the actual decline of dialect-speaking did not take off in earnest until after the Second World War (and, in many places, has remained only partial) the idea that the dialects might be harnessed for specialized literary purposes is an offshoot of the early twentieth-century vogue for seeking out new languages of art. The idea of dialect as an expressionistic literary device for the individual lyric poet—rather than the authentic collective voice of the people—comes from the very apex of the high modernist moment. It was the philosopher Benedetto Croce who, in Brevini's phrase, "baptized" the modernist theory of dialect writing.[19] The title alone of his 1926 essay "La letteratura dialettale in Italia e il suo significato" ("Dialect Literature in Italy and Its Meaning") already suggests a reflection on the medium as a signifier in itself. In this essay and in others, Croce was using ideas that had already been put forward by others in the late nineteenth century,[20] but he reframed them in more explicitly modernist terms. Central to his thought is the distinction between the unself-conscious, instinctive use of dialect as an automatic, reflex mode of expression, because it comes naturally, what Croce calls *uso spontaneo*, or "spontaneous use," and the deliberate decision to employ it instead of standard Italian, *uso riflesso*, "reflected use" or "deliberate use." The "spontaneous" use of dialect is characteristic of folk songs or local humorous poems, for example, and involves people composing verses in the language that comes most naturally to them and to their intended audience. "Reflected" use refers to the use of dialect by writers who would more instinctively have written in the literary standard, or whose audience is beyond the local range of the dialect; who use dialect as a formal device, or who write in dialect to make a point (political, poetic, or often both); that is, when the medium is part of the message. Or, to put it another way, when a writer chooses to write in dialect rather than in *a* dialect.

Croce's theories of the poetic possibilities dialects might offer are a definitive turning point between romantic and modernist conceptions of minor languages. The first Italian writer to put these theories into literary practice and to use dialect as a modernist tool was Pasolini. When he was born in 1922, it was still virtually a given that one was brought up speaking a dialect at home and in one's neighborhood, learning standard Italian at school as a language of writing and formal interactions. But because his parents were from different regions without a shared dialect, because the family moved around frequently during his childhood, and perhaps also because of his father's Fascist beliefs, the only language spoken in Pasolini's childhood home was standard Italian, and this was as a consequence Pasolini's only mother tongue. It is important to emphasize how uncommon this was in the Italy of the time. As Tullio De Mauro puts it, Pasolini "was one of the first Italian writers, perhaps the first major Italian writer, not to have had a native dialect, and to have been brought up speaking Italian from the start, something that, outside Tuscany and Rome, was, still in the 1940s, practiced only by a small number of families like his own, that is, families that were made up of parents from different regions and moved around [Pasolini è uno dei primi scrittori italiani, forse tra i maggiori il primo, che non abbia avuto un dialetto nativo, che sia stato educato a una precoce italofonia, quale quella che, fuori della Toscana e di Roma, ancora negli anni quaranta sperimentavano soltanto nuclei familiari come il suo, cioè di diversa composizione regionale e itineranti]."[21] One of the first writers not to have been a native speaker of *dialetto*, Pasolini was yet the first great modern writer of dialect poetry, devoting his first creative decade to writing poetry and drama in the dialects spoken in the Friuli region of northeastern Italy. This seeming contradiction is key to the meaning of his work, and it casts an interesting light on contemporaneous minor-language literary activity by nonnative speakers in distant countries, notably Ireland.

During the Second World War, the family sought refuge in the mother's home village of Casarsa, in the hills of Friuli, where Pasolini had spent many of the summers of his youth. Here he learned the local dialect from the neighbors. His artistic conversion to their language happened in a single instant, which he describes as follows:

> It was Livio, one of the Socolari boys, our neighbors across the street, who spoke. . . . The word "rosada" [dew] pronounced that sunny morning was nothing other than the expressive tip of his oral vitality.
>
> Certainly, that word, in all of the centuries it had been used in Friuli on this side of the Tagliamento river, *had never been written down*. It had always and only been *a sound*.
>
> [Era Livio, un ragazzo dei vicini oltre la strada, i Socolari, a parlare. . . . La parola "rosada" pronunciata in quella mattinata di sole, non era che una punta espressiva della sua vivacità orale.
>
> Certamente, quella parola, in tutti i secoli del suo uso nel Friuli che si stende al di qua del Tagliamento, *non era mai stata scritta*. Era stata sempre e solamente *un suono*.][22]

For Pasolini the point was not really writing but orality and spontaneity, the unselfconscious way the language existed, or seemed to exist, in the boy's body.[23] The contrast was with himself, for whom Friulian was not a native tongue, and therefore, to his way of seeing things, not naturally at home in his body. Pasolini was a rare writer for whom, to use Croce's vocabulary, the "spontaneous use" of dialect was literally impossible. Whatever miraculous qualities Pasolini discerned in the word "rosada" they were, by definition, invisible to Livio himself. It was the contrast between the total nativeness of the word to Livio and his body and its total outsideness to himself that struck Pasolini.

The day after his epiphany on hearing Livio utter the word "rosada," Pasolini sat down and wrote the poem "Il nìni muàrt" ("The Dead Boy"), often considered emblematic of his entire Friulian corpus, which it inaugurated. From then on, Pasolini switched to writing almost solely in Friulian. In 1942 he published, at his own expense, a collection of his poems in Friulian, *Poesie a Casarsa*. Many of these poems he had earlier drafted in Italian, but after his conversion he went back and translated them into Friulian, a process he referred to as "redialectizing" (*ridialettizzazione*).

It is a telling word, because it implies a *return* to dialect. But Pasolini was not really returning at all, he was venturing forth. By writing in Friulian, unlike writers of dialect in other places, he was not going back to the language of his early childhood or of his cherished family bonds but breaking away from them. This is a crucial point, as we shall see, for it brings together Pasolini's homosexuality, and his investment in queerness as an aesthetic point of view, with his fascination with dialect.

As Hideyuki Doi points out, it is impossible to place Pasolini's writing within the tradition of Friulian literary history in any meaningful way.[24] Instead, Pasolini's engagement with dialect in the 1940s is a logical extension of the modernist longing for a pure, private, poetic language. His imagination was captured not by Friulian itself so much as by the concept of dialect as a special form of authentic language of which he had been deprived, and whose lack he keenly felt in himself and in the world. He was inspired to write in dialect not because he possessed a dialect but because he felt he had lost it. Pasolini was one of the earliest witnesses, in his own life, to the psychological consequences of the loss of dialect, among the first to *feel* dialect as an absence, as a different form of language to be longed for, something that fed and was in turn fed by his own sensibility, thirsty for alternatives to the exhausted language of commodified, alienated modernity.

Pasolini is clear in his diaries that standard Italian—the language he had grown up in, the language of his home, of his relationship with his parents and his brother—was a *lingua grigia*, a "gray language," a sterile and bureaucratic invention, disconnected from authentic cultural or emotive life. Italian, although it was his own mother tongue, was not, he felt, capable of real life or nativeness. Friulian on the other hand seemed to him, as De Mauro puts it, "a bodily, physical reality, the carrier of an authentic tradition of life and culture [una realtà corposa, fisica, portatrice di una tradizione di vita e cultura autentica]."[25] At the time Pasolini was engaged in writing in it, Friulian showed no signs of falling out of popular use, but his

Friulian writing was a poetic vision that was intimately connected to the impending decline he (rightly) foresaw in the use of dialect in Italy.[26]

This concern with dialect as a distinct, and perhaps endangered, register of language—something Pasolini felt as an absence in himself—helped to create the literary idea of dialect in general. According to the most authoritative scholarship in the field, before Pasolini, the different dialects of Italy were unaware of literary activity in the others, other than perhaps Neapolitan.[27] Pasolini founded the Friulian Academy (Academiuta), but he was also passionately interested in the literary possibility of dialect in general, and through his energetic anthologizing was one of the first to really establish dialect poetry in Italy as a distinct strand of national literature. Because of Pasolini's intervention, the Italian dialects gradually became aware of a common literary cause. Pasolini was not only the first to fully exploit the modernist lyrical possibilities of dialect but also one of the instrumental figures in recognizing dialect in general as a poetic possibility in and of itself.

Yet Pasolini's commitment to the peasant lifeworld that dialect represented is in ways at odds with the ways he himself employed dialect in his poetry. However much he praised spoken Friulian as a source of human vitality and authenticity, he himself did not employ the living language for his poetry. The Friulian of *Poesie a Casarsa* is not written in any recognizable form of living Friulian but is rather a mixture of the previously unwritten dialect of Casarsa, the standard literary Friulian of Udine, deliberate archaisms, Italianisms, Hispanisms, and Provençalisms, a private language that did not correspond to any variety spoken by the inhabitants of Friuli. Pasolini later described his language in *Poesie a Casarsa* as "a form of absolute language, inexistent in nature [una specie di linguaggio assoluto, inesistente nella natura]."[28] Not only a language that nobody had written, as it turned out, but also one that nobody had ever spoken. Thus, while it was at first the *naturalness* of Friulian in the mouths of Livio and his fellow villagers, its apparently immanent connection to the natural landscape, that seemed to attract Pasolini to the language, in his own poetic compositions in Friulian he reshaped the forms of the living vernacular to make it unrecognizably alien from any form of the living language—in a way, as untethered from real life, people, and places as he could make it.

While apparently becoming as local as it is possible to be in a medium of poetic expression, Pasolini ultimately sought out the same paradox of readership that Joyce created with *Finnegans Wake*. The poems in *Poesie a Casarsa* were not written to be read by the native speakers of the village; in a sense they were not written to be read by anyone at all. It is not that he sought out a smaller audience, or even a tiny audience. The implied reader of *Poesie a Casarsa* is not an earthly one, not from an earthly place, *inesistente nella natura*.

The title of the collection thus takes on an ironic tinge. The pastoral and linguistic idyll that is supposedly identified with Casarsa and its people, supposedly a discovery of nature and vitality, is in fact a creation of some other supernatural world. This peculiar combination of a pastoral idyll and the ideal of a private poetic language can be found in "Il nìni muàrt" ("The Dead Boy"). It is striking that the poem, which was inspired by the sense of *aliveness* of the native language residing in the body and mind of a young boy, should be about a dead one. In its intertwining of life, death, nature, and the figure of Narcissus, the poem can be read as being about Pasolini's calling to writing in dialect. Without mentioning language at all, "The Dead Boy" deals with what the choice of dialect meant for Pasolini as a gay man, how it offered a means for expressing and investigating this predicament, this other way in which he was not "native" to the world. "The Dead Boy" can be read as also being about "the dead language," in the sense that for Pasolini, the seemingly native, living, linguistic world of dialect was "dead" to him.

> Bright evening, in the ditch
> the water is rising, a pregnant woman
> is walking in the field

I remember you, Narcissus, you had the color
of evening, when the bells
rang out with death.

[Sère imbarlumìde, tal fossâl
'a crès l'àghe, 'na fèmine plène
'a ciamìne tal ciamp

Jo ti ricuàrdi, Narcìs, tu vévis il colôr
da la sére, quànt lis ciampànis
'a sunin di muàrt.] (I.168)[29]

In the poem, the poet turns from the natural cycle of life and the
progress of time, represented by the pregnant woman, to the timeless
world of Narcissus staring at himself in the pool. The poem reflects
on language choice by turning away from embodiment and physical
presence, to a ghostly, disembodied, flickering image that cannot be
touched or held. The water in the womb, filled with a new body, is
replaced by the water of Narcissus's pool, filled with a disembodied
image of a body. In moving its gaze from the pregnant woman walking to the still, doubled image of the male narcissus, the poem also
hints at a turn away from heterosexuality, and from its temporality
of rebirth and movement, to "narcissistic" homosexuality and a different order of temporality, from the dynamic walking of the woman
and the future promised by her pregnancy, to memory, stillness, dou-
bling, to forms of reproduction that are imaginative or poetic but
not biological, not "natural." What Pasolini heard in the word "rosada" uttered by Livio Socolari was the miracle of embodied, truly
native language, of language, body, and self unconsciously at one.
The miracle is only visible, of course, to the nonnative speaker of the
language, to one in whom the language is *not* embodied.

For Pasolini, it felt as though he had no mother tongue, and his
exhilaration at hearing and watching Livio speak his native dialect
is that of witnessing the wonder of native language from one who
is excluded from it. But this idea, which Pasolini worked out, or
worked through, in the specific linguistic terms of Italy, dialect and
standard, was connected to a broader modernist sense of not being

native to language at all. It was also profoundly linked to Pasolini's homosexuality, to a gay predicament of feeling at odds with nature, an outsider to normal, natural rhythms of life, an alien even to one's own language.

The role of Pasolini's homosexuality in his imaginative projections around dialect is a complex question. Some scholars have suggested, partly in the light of his subsequent Roman career, that Pasolini's passion for Friulian dialects was a displaced version of a sexual curiosity for their speakers.[30] Certainly, his infatuation with the Friulian language went in tandem with his physical attraction to young Friulian men, but the linguistic component is more complex and more fundamental than a direct association between the young men he desired and the language they spoke.[31]

We are accustomed to thinking of queerness as a literary mode—like modernism—that goes together with the city. But the longings excited by dying rural vernaculars are bound up, almost structurally, with queerness. The connection becomes clearer when we compare Pasolini's Friulian with another case, that of the Irish writer Brendan Behan (1923–1964). Behan, a close contemporary of Pasolini from a thoroughly different culture and milieu, is a rare example of a somewhat openly gay or bisexual man in the Dublin of the 1940s. He also devoted a great part of his early career to writing in Irish. Although he was later known for his writing in English, between 1945 and 1950—the very same period in which Pasolini was engaged in his Friulian phase—Behan's reputation in Ireland rested entirely upon poems he published in Irish in various Irish-language journals. He stopped writing poetry abruptly after 1950 (coincidentally, just as Pasolini was forced, as we shall see, by a homosexual scandal to leave Friuli and its language behind forever). Behan's inner-city Dublin family could hardly have been further removed from Irish-speaking Ireland. He was taught the language by a fellow Irish Republican Army prisoner in Mountjoy, Seán Ó Briain, a native Irish speaker and schoolteacher from Baile an Fheirtéaraigh (Ballyferriter), an Irish-speaking parish close to Dún Chaoin, the Mecca of those writers and learners seeking authentic native Gaelic speech. Ó Briain introduced Behan to the classic poets Dáibhí Ó Bruadair and Brian Merriman, and to the Blasket island memoirs.[32] According to Ó Briain, Behan loved Tomás Criomhthain's *An tOileánach* (*The Islandman*) in particular and "loved to talk and learn about life in the Blaskets, Dún Chaoin and Ballyferriter."[33] He perfected his knowledge of the language under no less a tutor than Máirtín Ó Cadhain, again a fellow prisoner, when the pair were interned together in the Curragh camp (where Ó Cadhain was working on *Cré na Cille*).

In his biography of Behan, Ulick O'Connor wonders what the writer was seeking in or from the Irish language:

> Was Brendan persuaded by his political beliefs into writing in Irish? Or did he believe that through Irish he could come closer to his ancestral self than through English? Did he make the superb gesture and disdain an audience in the pursuit of his craft, working in silence at his artefact, seeking only its completion before turning to its successor?
>
> Was poetry in Irish a beginning for him, or a cul-de-sac? We shan't know. He stopped writing poetry after 1950.[34]

O'Connor has in mind here a nationalist-historical concept of a "self," and a patriotic view of why a writer might adopt Irish, the idea, which almost every native English-speaking Irish poet who has decided to write in Irish seems to share, that a "self" will find truer expression in the language of its ancestors. But given the fact that Behan first learned Irish from a cellmate, perfected it in the barracks of the Curragh internment camp, and that his masterpiece *Borstal Boy* is, in part, a touching evocation of a homoerotic attachment in prison, we might speculate that the longings Behan projected onto the Irish language were linked in some way to homosexuality.

The years in which Behan was active in the Irish language coincide with those in which he most actively pursued homoerotic affairs, mostly in an after-hours gathering place in the basement of a house at 13 Fitzwilliam Place, known as the Catacombs. For O'Connor, this concurrence suggests a personality split into two wholly opposed selves, a Gaelic self and a gay self: "The Catacombs," he writes, "were one side of Brendan's development as a writer at this time. He cultivated an entirely different side of himself when he went on visits to the Gaelic-speaking parts of Kerry."[35]

But if we set aside for a moment the national-historical context and the patriotic dimension of Behan's determination to learn and write in Irish, and think of him instead in relation to Pasolini and Friulian, it becomes clear that these two sides were not at all opposed, and that Behan's attachment to the Irish language and the Gaeltacht was an expression of queer desire. In the end, the homoerotic fumblings in the Catacombs and the high-minded trips to the Gaelic West—including frequent visits to Molly Ivors's Aran Islands—may for Behan have been really two sides of the same yearning for union and belonging. He wrote a poem in Irish in passionate praise of Oscar Wilde,[36] but more redolent of Pasolini's Friulian subjects was a poem dedicated to Seán Ó Briain, entitled "Jackeen ag Caoineadh na mBlascaod" ("A Jackeen [Dubliner] Lamenting the Blaskets"). This melancholy poem about the final depopulation of the Irish-speaking islands imagines the natural world around the Blaskets devoid of human presence:

> The great sea will be like glass under the sunset
> Without a boat sailing or any living sign of a person
> Just the last golden eagle up on the edge
> Of the world, above the lonely lying Blasket. . . .
>
> [Beidh an fharraige mhór faoi luí na gréine mar ghloine
> Gan bád faoi sheol ná comhartha beo ó dhuine
> Ach an t-iolar órga deireanach thuas ar imeall
> An domhain, thar an mBlascaod uaigneach luite. . . .][37]

The combination of the title and dedication of this poem—a Jackeen (a word which means a Dubliner, but also an urbanized, Anglicized Irish person) lamenting the desertion of the most emblematically rural and Irish-speaking community in Ireland—is redolent of Pasolini's position with regard to the youths, landscape, and language of Friuli. Unlike the Friulian of *Poesie a Casarsa*, there is little experimental or innovative about Behan's Irish, and it seems the two men did not know of one another's existence. For Pasolini and Behan, adopting a rural language of which they were not native speakers was a means to express a more generalized sense of not being at home in the world. For the two queer poets, idealizing this language, and fetishizing its native speakers, echoes with the predicament of gay people, of being on the outside looking in, foreigners in the "natural," organic world in which sexual desires are not singular, shameful internal states that set one apart from others but part of the unspoken order of things, a woman growing with child as naturally as the evening falls or the ditch fills with rainwater. Pasolini saw the nativeness of Friulians to their language and territory, and Behan the native speakers of south Connemara and west Kerry, in other words, as a gay man might fantasize either about heterosexuality, as a state in which one would be fully at home in the world, an insider to both society and nature, or of an alternative world in which homosexuality would be felt and lived as being at one with natural rhythms and the spontaneous cycle of life.

What appealed to Pasolini about Friulian was its apparently unself-conscious presence in the mouths of its speakers, its indissoluble connection to the place, people, and landscape, to the immanent rhythms of the natural world, something it seemed to him that neither his own mother tongue nor his sexuality could offer. In the Friulian dialects spoken in and around Casarsa—often unwritten forms—Pasolini found a language of authentic experience, in the words of Piera Rizzolati, "a paradise, a sort of linguistic Eden [un paradiso, una specie di Eden linguistico]."[38] The idea is a telling one, since what Eden represents in Genesis is first of all a world where sexuality is not marked, where sexual sin does not exist, a world where culture and nature are one. Pasolini's linguistic Eden was a sexual one as well: it represents, on the one hand, the (to the gay man's eyes) native rhythms of heterosexuality from which he is excluded but, on the other, the promise of undifferentiated sexual nativeness itself, a utopian world in which his own sexuality might be at home. The free and unself-conscious homoerotic behavior among Friulian adolescents in lakes and hedgerows, part of what Pasolini saw or imagined he saw in local life, was a crucial part of the organic, uncorrupted world that the language represented for him. For Pasolini, dialect and guiltless carnal pleasure remained closely linked. In his 1971 film *Il Decameron*, the use of dialect is associated with sinless sexual love.

Choosing Friulian as his creative medium allowed Pasolini, like Behan with Irish, not simply to express but to experience in a concentrated form his fundamental sense of not being native to the world. It allowed for nativeness to become visible and be experienced as a goal, it produced the notional possibility of a fuller, deeper, realer, more organic way of being in language and for language to relate to the lived world. Pasolini's homosexuality is at the heart of the odd paradox whereby he idealizes the nativeness of Friulian as a form of speech that seems to spring from nature, yet one that he remolds for his own poetic use into a synthetic version of it that no one in Casarsa or anywhere else had ever spoken. Pasolini's Friulian phase was a double-sided linguistic and poetic project, in which the two sides seem to be in conflict: of scrupulously, almost religiously rendering the spoken vernacular of the people, while transforming it into a created private language of the self—as a compromise between the internal fantasy, an inner utopia, and the real world where one longs to have this fantasy lived out in the flesh.

For Pasolini, the territory that corresponds to the language of *Poesie a Casarsa* is an imaginary one, an essence of nativeness located just beyond the world we inhabit but do not feel at home in. The etymology of *utopia* is the Greek *ou-topos* "not-place," or nowhere. "Jackeen ag Caoineadh na mBlascaod" suggests that, as we see in Pasolini, the poetic "white martyrdom" of moving from a major to a minor language, however much it appears to be compulsively fixated on real places and their inhabitants—Casarsa, the Blaskets, Dún Chaoin—in truth involves a longing for a world that is beyond human beings, a utopian construction of the mind, like Yeats's Byzantium.

The Pasolinis spoke only Italian at home. For the young Pier Paolo in Casarsa, Friulian was the language of his neighbors, a language spoken next door. Friulian was the sound of whatever world—erotic and otherwise—might lie beyond the intense, enveloping bonds of maternal love, beyond childhood and the nuclear family. For a gay man, whose sexuality cannot spontaneously (to borrow the term from Croce's linguistics) lead him to found a new, reproductive family home after the model of his childhood family, the call of the world beyond the birth family has a particular kind of force and intensity, something both alluring and unreachable.

A variety of longings, sexual and otherwise, a general sense of not being at home in the world, of not being fully native to it, underlay the desire of Pasolini to go nonnative and write in a minor language to which he had not been born. Like Behan, he idealized the locality where the language was spoken, as a rooted, solid reality in contrast to the rootless world of the major language he was native to. Pasolini's introductory poem to *Poesie a Casarsa* suggests what so many nonnative-speaking Irish-language writers would come to think about Dún Chaoin or Connemara—that by plumbing the inexhaustible well of language, he would also be plumbing the depths of his own soul:

> *Casarsa*
>
> Dedication.
> Spring of water of my village.
> There is no water fresher than that of my village.
> Spring of rustic love.
>
> [*Casarsa*
>
> Dedica.
> Fontana di aga dal me país.
> A no è aga pí fres-cia che tal me país.
> Fontana di rustic amòur.] (I.9)

But in the collection, Pasolini implicitly acknowledges the pure utopianism of this ideal of an earthly home for the soul by the expressionistic way in which he uses the local language in his poetry. By transforming the spoken language of the people, the language of Livio Socolari, into a private language of his own, he was accepting that the homeland cannot be fully or literally identified with a real place. It was a sense of outsiderness and exclusion, a longing for an elusive nativeness that drew him to Friulian in the first place. The impossibility of attaining this nativeness is further underlined by his invention of a personal form of the language not used in any real place or by any real people.

At the same time, Casarsa was not an arbitrary choice, and the desires projected onto it by Pasolini were also quite real. He did marvel at the unity of place, language, community, and self that he saw in Casarsa, and he did long to access this unity for himself; that this translated itself into sexual attraction for individuals is hardly surprising. The predicament of homosexuality in this situation is acutely analogous to the linguistic predicament. Nativeness, the state in Friulian dialects to which Pasolini could, through study and practice, come ever closer but could never fully reach, becomes a promised land of true belonging just beyond the horizon of lived experience; for a gay man it resonates with the problem of how to mature, the problem of a sexuality that does not allow one to become "native" to the world beyond the birth family.[39] Pasolini can never attain the natural, unconscious, native belonging in the local dialect that he thinks he sees and hears in the youths of Casarsa; this nativeness is, by definition, invisible to them, but will always be visible to him, no matter how deeply he embeds himself within it. Just as he cannot ever fully "go native" linguistically, he cannot do so sexually either.

For all the knowledge and for all the explicit statements and indeed actions that acknowledge Casarsa as a *paese dell'anima*, a landscape of the soul, and its language as a personal poetic instrument, Pasolini was driven by a real, immediate desire to become native, to connect intimately, bodily, with Casarsa and with the handsome young men of Friuli. His engagement with the Friulian language was a mixture of poetic and personal longings, a desire of both the soul and the flesh, and the villages and people of Friuli were a combination of inner projections and external realities he wanted to be part of. The *rustic amòur* of the poem is both an idea and an immediate, fleshly, *embodied* reality.

His learning and use of the language, and the vision of native perfection, bodily freedom and happiness that Pasolini saw embodied by the language were central to this longing. And indeed, the struggle between his inner utopian Friuli, the *paese dell'anima*, landscape of the soul, and the real concrete place and its people, played itself out in the linguistic sphere. As Pasolini's time in Friuli went on through the 1940s, the undefinable longings woven into his private, delocalized Friulian idiolect became more and more mapped onto the concrete specifics of the locality. His later Friulian writing is not in an invented version of the language but composed in actual local micro-varieties of Friulian *caint na ndaoine*, "speech of the people," meticulously, indeed obsessively, reconstructed. He revised *Poesie a Casarsa*, "translating" his private language into an exact rendering of the dialect spoken by the people of Casarsa (for some of the poems, their third linguistic existence). His later Friulian poetry had sections labeled with the name of the village where its notional speaker was from. The faithfulness with which he reproduced the minutiae of spoken varieties of language impressed even dialectologists.[40]

Pasolini's program initially corresponds to ideas expressed by Seán Ó Ríordáin (the subject of the next chapter) in an essay entitled "Teangacha Príobháideacha" ("Private Languages"), in which Ó Ríordáin suggests that all instantiations of Irish can be considered expressions of a single, underlying ur-Irish, a sort of spirit—*meanma*—of which each micro-variety is a manifestation, but which is not graspable in any actualized iteration.[41] While Ó Ríordáin is saying that this *meanma* lurks beneath all varieties, the implication is that it is also always just out of sight and reach. Between *Poesie a Casarsa* and his later poems in dialect, Pasolini struggled to transform the utopia into a real place, from *ou-topos* to *topos*. As Pasolini's idea of Friulian became increasingly identified with the actual place and people of Casarsa and its environs, as the balance tipped between internal vision and external reality, as Friulian became less a disembodied private language and more identified with physical places, he also tried to reembody the longed-for *meanma*, the underlying perfect spirit of the language, in actual sexual encounters.

As Pasolini attempted to map the idealized sexual paradise he perceived in the language onto the real people who spoke it and the actual place in which it was spoken, the gap between spoken varieties of language and the *meanma* they evoked, between the embodied place and people and the disembodied ideal of nativeness, between the abstract, spiritual, and political promises of *rustic amòur* and the bodily aspect of love became brutally tangible. In 1949, some teenage boys were overheard discussing a sexual incident that had taken place in the woods with the writer during a local festival. Word spread; the police were informed; since Pasolini was head teacher in the local school, his position was untenable, and he fled to Rome with his mother. He was banished from his linguistic and sexual Eden. The yearning for a paradise of sexual and linguistic oneness was frustrated, and the isolation that had led him to the fantasy in the first place ended up being painfully reconfirmed by it. In Rome he began a new phase of his career, eventually switching his sexual and spiritual focus onto a new minor language, working-class Roman dialect.[42]

The twentieth-century fate of minor languages and dialects, nowhere more so than in Italy and Ireland, suggests that to write in a dead or dying language may be not only an imposition but also a deep poetic desire, even necessity. It was Giovanni Pascoli himself, in some ways the poetic forerunner of Pasolini, who speculated that "the language of poetry is always a dead language [la lingua della poesia è sempre una lingua morta]."[43] Even though Friulian was still vibrant as a community language when Pasolini came to it, the vision he found in it was absolutely linked to the imagined prospect of its vernacular decline. The concurrence of the vernacular demise of the dialects and their poetic blossoming is not a tragic or ironic coincidence, nor an example of mere belatedness—something not valued until it is about to be lost—but a relationship of consequence. It was in the 1960s and 1970s, long after Pasolini's engagement with Friulian was over, that standard Italian began really to compete with and supplant dialect as the instinctive language of colloquial and intimate purposes in most of Italy. Pasolini's Friulian is the founding moment for the later and much more widespread diffusion of neodialect poetry in Italy from the 1970s, a literary blossoming that coincided with the regression of spoken dialects and the emergence, for the first time in Italian history, of a shared spoken national language.[44]

For these later writers, such as Andrea Zanzotto, Tonino Guerra, and Amedeo Giacomini, the turn to dialect was in part a reaction to the despoilment and degradation of older ways of life they had known in their youth, which included dialect. As John P. Welle points out, in the late 1950s and 1960s (when Pasolini had left behind his own Friulian phase), Zanzotto was still writing only in standard Italian, and it would be another decade before he adopted his native Venetian dialect of Soligo as a literary medium.[45]

But Pasolini differs from, for example, Zanzotto in his original outsiderness to dialect, his historically premature nativeness to standard Italian. His linguistic biography underlines how the concept of a lost language not only reflects concrete sociohistorical reality in postwar Italy but is also an artistic ideal: an autonomous, time-proof realm of pure poetry, and a fantasy that this poetic paradise might be found on earth. Pasolini himself wrote, reflecting on what he had been doing with Friulian: "It was even possible to invent an entire linguistic system, a private language . . . and . . . to find it already physically ready-made, and with what splendor, in dialect [Era addirittura possibile inventare un intero sistema linguistico, una lingua privata . . . trovandola . . . fisicamente già pronta, e con quale splendore, nel dialetto]."[46]

This idea has striking, indeed revolutionary, consequences if we apply it to twentieth-century Ireland. As much as Pasolini's linguistic biography and its literary ramifications in the 1940s casts interesting light on the Italian neodialect movement in poetry at the very end of the twentieth century, it turns out to be extraordinarily revealing in understanding the development of Irish-language literature, where the production, by second-language speakers, of literary texts, has been wrongly been assimilated to the battle to save or resuscitate the spoken language and help the nation return to it.

Seán Ó Ríordáin (1917–1977), a close contemporary of Pasolini, is the key canonical figure in twentieth-century Irish-language poetry, and the most controversial.[1] The first poet to write recognizably modern lyric poetry in Irish, he is often said to be the most accomplished writer of Irish since Aogán Ó Rathaille (1670–1728). A single poem by Ó Ríordáin, "Adhlacadh mo Mháthar" ("My Mother's Burial"), published in 1945, is widely considered to have inaugurated modern lyric poetry in Irish, and to have instantly changed the literary possibilities of the language. Ó Ríordáin's poetry represents in many ways some of the hopes bound up in the language revival: that the national language, which survived British rule as native speech only in scattered pockets, might yet be born again as a great literary vehicle and as the language of a modern European nation. Yet Ó Ríordáin always felt himself to be an outsider to native Irish, and over the course of his lifetime he witnessed its ongoing, in some ways accelerated, decline as an everyday spoken language. Ó Ríordáin wrote only in Irish, but he did not consider himself a native speaker, and his choice was a source of unalleviated suffering and bitter self-recrimination. Writing Irish, as he often admitted in his diaries, was a torture for him, but it was the only language he ever used for creative purposes. His poetry was praised for bringing modern techniques for the first time to Irish-language literature, but it was criticized by some for what they considered to be the inauthentic, artificial, even incorrect quality of his Irish.

The paradoxes of Ó Ríordáin's career and the meaning of his decision to write in Irish are cast in a new light when we consider Ó Ríordáin after Pasolini. Pasolini, an openly gay Marxist, who sought inspiration among pimps and petty criminals and revolutionized modern Italian culture and European cinema, seems a most unlikely term of comparison for Ó Ríordáin, a conservative, sickly recluse, beset with Catholic scruples, who produced only a few slim volumes of verse in the course of his quiet life on the outskirts of Cork. But Pasolini's poetic investment in dialect allows us to understand the paradoxes at the heart of Ó Ríordáin's career in a revelatory way, and to see his vexed relationship to Irish not as an incidental handicap but as central to his unique vision.

Dialetto has been the subject of long reflection in Italy as a purely poetic register, unlike Irish in Ireland, whose use as a poetic medium has been conflated with cultural politics and the nationalist language revival. By comparing Pasolini's use of dialect with Ó Ríordáin's use of Irish, my aim is not to set up a general framework of comparison between the longer linguistic history of the two countries; still less is it to suggest a noble shared predicament of plucky minor languages bravely battling for survival against an oppressive major-language foe. Instead, placing the two contemporaneous but apparently divergent literary moments together reveals the outlines of a common mid-century phenomenon of seeking in minor languages an outlet of expression for earlier, modernist dreams.

Ó Ríordáin and Pasolini were not aware of each other, and Ó Ríordáin never said, as Pasolini wrote about Friulian, that in adopting Irish he was looking for a corresponding external equivalent for a private internal ideal of language. He viewed his strange way of writing Irish as a stylistic sensibility *within* the ongoing history of the Irish language, a way of helping a continuous tradition to advance. His reputation in Irish-language literature is as a kind of patriotic Prometheus, who, despite the pain and sacrifice he underwent to do so, brought modern literary techniques from outside to the Irish language. Considering Ó Ríordáin alongside Pasolini, however, suggests that the dynamic might have been the reverse: that Ó Ríordáin did not give the gift of literary modernity to Irish, but rather, in its ruined state and in his own ambiguous, angst-ridden relationship to it, Irish gave an expression of modernity to Ó Ríordáin.

Pasolini's statement about his use of Friulian can adjusted to describe Ó Ríordáin's decision to write in Irish: that it seemed possible "to invent an entire linguistic system, a private language . . . and . . . to find it already physically ready-made, and with what splendour, in the Irish language."[2] When applied to the Irish language reflections such as this one suggest that some strains of the practice of writing in Irish in the twentieth century can be viewed as a form of expressionism, leaving us with the almost scandalous idea that Ó Ríordáin's choice of Irish might be viewed less as a patriotic dedication to the cause of the language, and more as a "technique," of a piece with the experiments of surrealism, futurism, and other experimental aesthetic movements.

When Ó Ríordáin was born in 1917, Irish-speaking territories could be found in counties Cork, Clare, Kerry, Donegal, Galway, Waterford, and Mayo. In addition, patches of native speech, or at least surviving heritage speakers, could still be found in most counties in the island. By the time he died, in 1977, there were almost no native speakers left of dialects outside the official Gaeltacht, and the true Gaeltacht itself had contracted significantly. Ó Ríordáin's own early life and his own aesthetic vision were not a glorious contradiction or exception to this decline but were intimately bound up with it, and the late modernist vision that he was able to articulate through the Irish language—and only through the Irish language—was inseparable from the language's demise as a vernacular.

Like Pasolini, Ó Ríordáin had a complex linguistic biography that is crucial to understanding his poetic project. He was born in Baile Bhuirne (sometimes spelled Baile Mhuirne; called Ballyvourney in English), a village in the Muskerry region of northwest Cork. The language had clung to these hills for longer than in most parts of the country, and when the 1926 Gaeltacht Commission issued its findings, the western part of Muskerry, including Baile Bhuirne, was recommended for inclusion, even though in Baile Bhuirne the shift from Irish to English was already irreversibly under way.

The transition came so late to Baile Bhuirne that it avoided the traumatic rupture that had characterized the panicked switch to English in areas such as Tumgesh, anglicized a generation or two earlier, whereby a generation who had never spoken or known any language but Irish had had found itself suddenly stranded in a sea of English. The language transition was a more peaceful and orderly affair in Baile Bhuirne, a slowly shifting bilingualism of a sort that never existed in Tumgesh, a gradual but steady drift from Irish and English to English and Irish (or, to put it another way, from Irish at home and English in school to English at home and Irish in school). In Ó Ríordáin's youth, almost everyone knew both languages, but different generations used them for different purposes. The census returns show only a handful of monoglots of either language in the area in 1901 and 1911. Ó Ríordáin himself knew of only one local person in his childhood who could not speak English, and, conversely, most of the habitual English speakers knew Irish well. Even though some of his defenders have felt the need to insist on Ó Ríordáin's credentials as a native speaker of Irish,[3] Ó Ríordáin himself was explicit and definite—and anguished— about the fact that he was not. His mother, who had married into the area from an English-speaking district, was unusual in Baile Bhuirne in knowing no Irish at all. His father was from the village and was a native speaker of Irish, but he did not use Irish with his own children, and the sole language of the household was English. He died of tuberculosis when Ó Ríordáin was ten, removing the last potential, if never actualized, link with native Irish within the household.

Ó Ríordáin's chief exposure to the language came from visits he would pay to his father's mother and sister, Ó Ríordáin's grandmother and his aunt Han, who lived next door, and to the house of another elderly neighbor, Nell Mhattie, to listen to them and their friends talking and singing. In his own account of these visits, Ó Ríordáin cuts a strangely passive figure—he would listen to stories and songs and conversations, and ask questions, but there is little sense of his being an active participant. After his father's death, Ó Ríordáin would visit partly out of an eagerness to hear about his father's youth. In his visits next door, the young Ó Ríordáin seems to be trying to reinhabit the place of his father, nourishing simultaneously his Irish and his knowledge of his dead father—and, especially, his knowledge of his father's life before and outside the family.

Ó Ríordáin's relationship to Irish and thus the particular poetic possibilities it gave him could only have come from a place like Baile Bhuirne. When he recalled the different ways the two languages of the village imprinted themselves on his childhood mind, he recalled that Irish and English were associated not only with different generations but also with different realms of feeling and experience, English the language of daytime, and Irish a language of the night (a reflection that gives the present book its title):

> I was born in the Gaeltacht. The Ballyvourney Gaeltacht was already very patchy at that time. It was easy to see which language would win out. Irish was retreating. It was retreating into the remote places. The main road and the village of Carraig an Adhmaid were English-speaking. Irish was retreating within the minds of the old people. You associated it with old people, even though young and old all knew Irish well. There was some wealth in what Irish was there, but it was becoming scarce. There was nobody as far as I know except for an old woman in Gort Uí Raithile who could only speak Irish. . . . And Irish was retreating into the night. It was mostly at night that you would hear the Irish of the old people, and you associated the language with the night.
>
> [San Ghaeltacht a rugadh me. Bhí Gaeltacht Baile Mhúirne breac go maith an uair úd. B'fhuirist a thuiscint cé aige a bheadh an lá. Bhí an Ghaeilge ag cúladh. Bhí sí ag cúladh isteach ins na áiteanna iargúltha. Bhí an bóthar mór agus sráidbhaile Charraig an Adhmaid fén mBéarla. Bhí sí ag cúladh isteach in intinn na seandaoine. Is le seandaoine a shamhlofá í, cé go raibh Gaeilge mhaith ag óg agus aosta. Bhí mianach in a raibh ann di, ach bhí sí ag fáil gann. Ní raibh aoinne go bhfios domhsa ach seanabhean i nGort Uí Raithile a bhí i dtaoibh le Gaeilge amháin. . . . Agus bhí an Ghaeilge ag cúladh isteach san oíche. Istoíche isea is mó a chloisfeá Gaeilge na seandaoine, agus is leis an oíche a shamhlófí an teanga.][4]

The clarity with which Ó Ríordáin writes about the linguistic environment of his boyhood in Baile Bhuirne is striking in comparison with the "great silence" that surrounds the subject in places like

Tumgesh. At the same time, the distinction between native and non-native speakers of the language in Baile Bhuirne was clear and important. Ó Ríordáin emphasizes in his diaries that, unlike the case with his grandmother, aunt, and father, English was the language he had been brought up in, the language he spoke most naturally and most often in his own life. He fretted openly about his level of Irish, worked to improve it, considered the fact that he was not a native speaker to be a terrible deficiency, and envied the native ability of others.[5] In a letter to Donncha Ó Laoghaire he writes that it was "a cause of despair as well as happiness to listen the people in Dún Chaoin [that is, native speakers from a living Gaeltacht] speaking Irish."[6] In 1961, as he was reading Máirtín Ó Direáin's essay collection *Feamainn Bhealtaine* (*May Seaweed*) with a mixture of admiration and jealous pain, he wrote of his own writing in Irish:

> I am tired of this dead speech! I would prefer English itself. Is it my native language not English? The language I spoke when I was a child, the language I have mostly spoken in the course of my life. All I have seen and experienced is tied up with English. What bad luck did I have the first day I started with Irish?
>
> [Táim tuirseach den gcaint mharbh so! B'fhearr Béarla féin. Nach í mo theanga dhúchais í an Béarla? An teanga a labhras agus mé im leanbh, an teanga is mó a labhras i gcaitheamh mo shaoil. Is tríthi atá a bhfuil den mbeatha feicthe agus blaiste agamsa fite fuaite. Cad é an mí-ádh a bhí orm an chéad lá dul le Gaeilge?][7]

As a child in Baile Bhuirne Ó Ríordáin was close to Irish but not intimate with it. Schooling had been in Irish, friendship and play in English; the language of his own hearth was English, but one house and one generation removed, Irish prevailed; English was the language of his mother and his siblings, alive and struggling together, of work and youth and life, the language of the daytime, while Irish was the language of the night, of the dead and the old, of his distant, and later deceased, father, of his elderly grandmother, and of the vanished world before his own birth that those two had shared, a mother-son bond parallel with his own. In a late essay, reflecting on his command of Irish and how it had evolved over the course of his life, Ó

Ríordáin wrote that when he was a child in Baile Bhuirne, while they spoke English at home, Irish was "ag béal an dorais," "next door."[8] He meant this in the literal sense that it was the language he heard and spoke when he visited his grandmother or Nell Mhattie, but it was true in a metaphorical and psychological sense too: at home Irish was a silent language buried within his father's mind and memories, never used in the family. Irish was never at home, and conversely Ó Ríordáin was himself not "at home" in Irish.

The Baile Bhuirne of Ó Ríordáin's youth was in some senses a symbolic encapsulation of the linguistic psychology of the state: while the lives of young people and the ordinary, day-to-day affairs of the village were conducted in English, Irish was the language of the old and—this being a key difference between Baile Bhuirne and places like Tumgesh—Irish remained as the language of "high culture" in the area, both because of its central position in the school system and because it was retained as the language of poetry and songs.[9] The English spoken in the district, barely two generations old, was in Ó Ríordáin's opinion a deracinated and impoverished creole. It certainly was heir to no established cultural tradition with which its speakers could identify. The older native Irish speakers, such as Ó Ríordáin's paternal grandmother, on the other hand, had access to the remains of the older sophisticated oral tradition, and thus to cultural riches not available in the rough English of the village, but for Ó Ríordáin with his school Irish they were out of reach, always "next door."[10] As the older generation aged and died, and their children, such as Ó Ríordáin's father, stopped speaking the language of their own youth, native Irish was quickly disappearing.

When Ó Ríordáin was fifteen the gap between him and native Irish was further widened when his mother moved the family out of Muskerry to Inniscarra, on the outskirts of Cork city, firmly in English-speaking Ireland. The presence of Irish as the language next door thereafter became a purely metaphorical one. After school, Ó Ríordáin obtained a permanent post as a clerk in the Motor Taxation Office in Cork city. To the fragments of native speech that had littered his Baile Bhuirne childhood—the ruins of what had been his father's boyhood world—by now had been added the official language of the revival and of the state bureaucracy, first through school and later through his job as a civil servant, where he would have been confronted daily with bilingual official forms and notices, and where several of his (mother-tongue English) colleagues were active members of the Gaelic League (Conradh na Gaeilge as it was now known).[11]

Ó Ríordáin lived in Inniscarra for the rest of his life, commuting daily the few miles to Cork, working in City Hall by day as Jackie Riordan—the name with which he had been brought up, and by which he was always known to his family and colleagues—and composing poems in Irish by night in Inniscarra as Seán Ó Ríordáin. That Ó Ríordáin's English "day name," the identity which he inhabited in the minds of most of those who knew him intimately, has not survived is in itself a telling comment on the poetry: Jackie Riordan and his daily life (in English) were condemned to be excluded from it.

This double life was central to Ó Ríordáin's adult view of himself and his art. In his diaries he describes the bridge between Inniscarra and Cork as a passage between two worlds, and it is this aspect of his linguistic biography—bureaucracy in English by day in Cork, and poetry in Irish by night in Inniscarra—that commentators have often seized upon as the key to Ó Ríordáin. Ó Ríordáin's account of this binary, moving between soulless official English and human, poetic Irish, is enthusiastically accepted perhaps partly due to the fact that it reverses what is the usual experience of the two languages for Irish people, Irish in school and on official forms, English in social and intimate interactions. But Ó Ríordáin had a rich emotional life in English in Cork. He was a frequent visitor to the house of his brother Tadhg, whose children remember "Uncle Jackie" as an affectionate and playful presence. Ó Ríordáin's diaries record a real attachment to Tadhg's children, an experience of love and connection that is largely absent from the anguished Irish-language poetry, in which, as Seán Ó Tuama points out, he rarely mentions another person, other than, occasionally, his mother. His co-workers remember "Mr. Riordan" as a witty, humorous colleague,[12] and his letters to them, especially to Séamus Ó Coigligh and Con Prior, are full of warm declarations of attachment and affection.

In a letter from Heatherside sanatorium to Ó Coigligh, Ó Ríordáin gives a passionate account of how central his friendships in City Hall are to his life, and especially the friendship with Ó Coigligh himself: "By C[ity] H[all], I mean K[ay] F[oley], you, Con Prior, Bill Daly and Miss Hanrahan. K.F. As for yourself, when I think of yourself traveling through different languages . . . I think I would die if you were not there. ['Sé an bhrí atá agamsa le H[alla] na C[athrach] ná K[ay] F[oley], tusa, Con Prior, Bill Daly agus Miss Hanrahan . . . Maidir leatsa, nuair a chuimhním ort agus tú ag taisteal trés na teangachaibh . . . measaim go bhfaighinn bás dá mba ná beifeá ann.]"[13]

This letter is in Irish, but the social life Ó Ríordáin refers to in City Hall was in English, and almost all of his intimate and social life was in English.[14] In fact, if he felt he could not write poetry in English, he also felt that he could not have authentic human relationships in Irish. In his diaries, he lambasted the artificiality and pretension of his efforts to speak Irish in daily life with other nonnative speakers. Not long after his despairing entry about his own "dead speech" compared to the Irish of native speakers, he wondered after meeting a fellow enthusiast for dinner in Cork city if their awkward insistence on speaking Irish to one another when they were both native speakers of English was a form of dishonesty, even of insanity:

Are we mad, urban *Gaeilgeoirí* [Irish language revivalists] in an English-speaking city? Is it even worse than that? Are we dishonest—even with ourselves? Have we refused to face the truth? If we were native speakers of Irish recently arrived from the Gaeltacht, that might be another story. But the two of us have lived most of our lives through English and now we come to the Buffet and we speak Irish in public—faulty Irish.

[An dream buile sinne, Gaeilgeoirí cathrach, i gcathair le Béarla? An measa ná san é? An bhfuilimid mímhacánta—fiú amháin linn féin? An

bhfuil diúltaithe againn aghaidh a thabhairt ar an bhfírinne? Dá mba
Ghaeilgeoirí dúchais sinn aniar ón nGaeltacht le gairid, ba scéal eile é,
déarfá. Ach beirt sinn a chaitheann an chuid is mó dá saol trí Bhéarla
agus ansan tagaimid go dtí an Buffet agus labhraimid Gaeilge go poiblí—Gaeilge lochtach.][15]

Writing in Irish was a lonely and painful calling for Ó Ríordáin,
and cultural nationalism alone is not a sufficient explanation for why
he chose to do so. Most of his detractors and supporters alike take it
for granted that the closeness of his childhood exposure to the native
language in his grandmother's and neighbors' houses was his greatest
asset as an Irish-language poet, and the distance yet remaining between him and the language—if it was there at all, and plenty of his
defenders said there was none—his greatest flaw. But I want to suggest in what follows that it was exactly this distance that Irish offered
Ó Ríordáin. Certainly, the linguistic predicament in which his choice
of medium placed him for his career—being close to, yet just at one
remove from native Irish, and being in the position of constantly,
tirelessly endeavoring to eliminate this unbridgeable distance—must
have had powerful resonances with the psychological linguistic terrain of his childhood in Baile Bhuirne.[16]

This is not to deny the force of Ó Ríordáin's cultural nationalism,
which was the obvious surface component of his determination to
write in the national language. He seems really to have believed that
there was nothing of any value in Ireland outside the Gaeltacht. According to the historian John A. Murphy, who knew him, Ó Ríordáin
considered English-speaking Ireland to be a "desert" and felt that
English-speaking towns in Ireland were "as good as dead" in comparison with the living Gaeltacht of Dún Chaoin.[17] The decline in the
extent and quality of native spoken Irish in Ireland that he witnessed
in his lifetime was a cause of great sorrow to Ó Ríordáin, a commit-
ted cultural nationalist. But if this cultural degradation—as he saw
it—angered and depressed him on a conscious level, on a poetic level,
the twilit half-life of the Irish language in the mid-twentieth century
offered him a valuable tool. In Baile Bhuirne (unlike Tumgesh) when

Ó Ríordáin was a child, local native Irish and revivalist school Irish had coincided and coexisted side by side. Just as Pasolini was among the first Italian writers to feel in himself the consequences of the loss of dialect, Ó Ríordáin, for whom native Irish was so close and in evidence but just out of reach, experienced in an immediate, visceral way the loss of vernacular Irish and the deterritorialization of the language.

His first collection, *Eireaball Spideoige* (*A Robin's Tail*) appeared in 1952 to both acclaim and great controversy. There was no doubt about its poetic power and ambition, but the kind of Irish it was written in, stretched and pulled, partly by English, into unrecognizable forms, was not like any Irish anyone had ever seen or spoken before. *Eireaball Spideoige* did not just express, belatedly, a modernist sensibility through the medium of the Irish language, it changed at a stroke the way in which the language could be used. Influenced by Rimbaud, Yeats, Eliot, and especially his fellow Catholic, Gerard Manley Hopkins, Ó Ríordáin invented abstract compound words and drew on imagery and a metaphorical vocabulary that were wholly alien to the Irish tradition.[18]

The Burial of English

Máire Mhac an tSaoi, Ó Ríordáin's most scathing detractor, accused him of failing to respect the fact that Irish was a living language. This criticism upset him greatly, since he had such envy and respect for native speakers. But in Ó Ríordáin's experience of Irish and English, "life" and "death" have complex meanings. English was the language of at-homeness and physical presence, and Irish the language of a dead parent, and of his lost world, of the world next door. The fascination of Irish for Ó Ríordáin—the language his father had grown up in but never spoke at home—was bound up with this early loss of his father. Given this background, it is fitting that Ó Ríordáin's first major poem—the poem that is credited, on its own, with plunging Irish-language literature into the modern era—is about death. But the death it addresses, ostensibly at least, is not that of his father but that of his mother.

Ó Tuama writes that "Adhlacadh mo Mháthar" ("My Mother's Burial") "astonished those whose reading in Irish had hitherto been confined to traditional literature. . . . [As] Baudelaire. . . . created a new 'frisson' in French poetry . . . Ó Ríordáin . . . in his day, created a new 'frisson' in Gaelic-Irish literature with the publication of this poem."[19] The poem is a description of the poet's attempt to fully inhabit the reality of this mother's death at her funeral, and its treatment of this subject has made it one of the most famous poems in modern Irish. The poem is justly renowned for its revolutionary use of Irish, but we can also read it, like Pasolini's "Il nìni muàrt" ("The Boy Dies"), as a poem about the poetic decision to write in a nonnative language, not only "the burial of my mother" but also "the burial of my mother tongue."[20]

> *My Mother's Burial*
> The June sun in an orchard,
> And a rustling in the silk of the afternoon,
> A cursed bee lilting
> A screamrip in the nooncloak.
>
> I reading a dirtied old letter,
> With every worddrop I drank
> A furious pain piercing my breast,
> Every one of those words squeezed out its own tear.
>
> I remembered the hand that did the writing,
> A hand that was as familiar as a face.
> A hand that proffered kindness like an old Bible,
> A hand that was like a balm when you were sick.
>
> And June fell back into winter,
> The orchard was turned into a white graveyard by a river,
> And in the midst of the dumbwhite around me
> The darkhole screamed out loud in the snow,
>
> The white of a young girl on the day of her First Communion,
> The white of the host on the altar on a Sunday,

The white of milk trickling from the breasts,
When they buried my mother, the white of the ground.

My mind was whipping itself, trying
To taste the burial fully,
When through the white silence there gently flew
A robin, unconfused and unafraid:

And it waited over the grave as though it knew
That the reason that had brought it was hidden to all
Except for the person who was waiting in the coffin,
And I was jealous of the unusual fellowship.

The air of Heaven descended on that grave,
The bird was possessed by a holy, terrible mirth,
I was cut off, a layman, from the mysterious business,
In that grave far away in front of me.

The fragrance of sorrow filled my debauched soul,
The snow of virginity fell on my heart,
Now I will bury in that heart made honest
The memory of the woman who carried me three seasons in her womb.

The gravediggers came with the rough noise of shovels,
And vigorously swept the clay into the grave,
I looked the other way, a neighbor was wiping his knees,
I looked at the priest and there was worldliness in his face.

The June sun in an orchard,
And a rustling in the silk of the afternoon,
A cursed bee lilting
A screamrip in the nooncloak.

I write lame little rhymes,
I would like to catch a robin's tail,
I would like to banish the spirit of knee-wipers,
I would like to journey to the end of the day in sorrow.

[*Adhlacadh mo Mháthar*

Grian an Mheithimh in úllghort,
Is siosarnach i síoda an tráthnóna,
Beach mhallaithe ag portaireacht
Mar screadstracadh ar an nóinbhrat.

86

Seanalitir shalaithe á léamh agam,
Le gach focaldeoch dár ólas
Pian bhinibeach ag dealgadh mo chléibhse,
Do bhrúigh amach gach focal díobh a dheoir féin.

Do chuimhníos ar an láimh a dhein an scríbhinn,
Lámh a bhí inaitheanta mar aghaidh,
Lámh a thál riamh cneastacht seana-Bhíobla,
Lámh a bhí mar bhalsam is tú tinn.

Agus thit an Meitheamh siar isteach sa Gheimhreadh,
Den úllghort deineadh reilig bhán cois abhann,
Is i lár na balbh-bháine i mo thimpeall
Do liúigh os ard sa tsneachta an dúpholl,

Gile gearrachaile lá a céad chomaoine,
Gile abhlainne Dé Domhnaigh ar altóir,
Gile bainne ag sreangtheitheadh as na cíochaibh,
Nuair a chuireadar mo mháthair, gile an fhóid.

Bhí m'aigne á sciúirseadh féin ag iarraidh
An t-adhlacadh a bhlaiseadh go hiomlán,
Nuair a d'eitil tríd an gciúnas bán go míonla
Spideog a bhí gan mhearbhall gan scáth:

Agus d'fhan os cionn na huaighe fé mar go mb'eol di
Go raibh an toisc a thug í ceilte ar chách
Ach an té a bhí ag feitheamh ins an gcomhrainn,
Is do rinneas éad fén gcaidreamh neamhghnách.

Do thuirling aer na bhFlaitheas ar an uaigh sin,
Bhí meidhir uafásach naofa ar an éan,
Bhíos deighilte amach ón diamhairghnó im thuata,
Is an uaigh sin os mo chómhair in imigéin.

Le cumhracht bróin do folcadh m'anam drúiseach,
Thit sneachta geanmnaíochta ar mo chroí,
Anois adhlacfad sa chroí a deineadh ionraic
Cuimhne na mná d'iompair mé trí ráithe ina broinn.

Tháinig na scológa le borbthorann sluasad,
Is do scuabadar le fuinneamh an chré isteach san uaigh,

D'fhéachas sa treo eile, bhí comharsa ag glanadh a ghlúine,
D'fhéachas ar an sagart is bhí saoltacht ina ghnúis.

Grian an Mheithimh in úllghort,
Is siosarnach i síoda an tráthnóna,
Beach mhallaithe ag portaireacht
Mar screadstracadh ar an nóinbhrat.

Ranna beaga bacacha á scríobh agam,
Ba mhaith liom breith ar eireaball spideoige,
Ba mhaith liom sprid lucht glanta glún a dhíbirt,
Ba mhaith liom triall go deireadh an lae go brónach.]

Ó Tuama writes that with the first four lines of the poem alone we
enter an exciting "milieu which poetry in Irish had never entered."[21]
The phrase "siosarnach i síoda an tráthnóna," "a rustling in the silk
of the afternoon," is the line most often cited as summing up what
was new and surprising in Ó Ríordáin's way of writing Irish. The image may seem straightforward and even tame in translation to someone used to modern poetry in English or French, but nothing like it
in Irish had ever been attempted before. In a long essay praising the
poem (criticizing only its last line as a partly unsuccessful attempt to
imitate Eliot's device of bathos), Ó Tuama gives a detailed explanation of the various ways in which the phrase comes out of a worldview alien to the Irish language (its fundamentally English origin can
be more clearly intuited, he suggests, if we translate it as "a rustling
in the noonday silk"). Ó Tuama writes that for the Irish-speaking
reader the phrase "leaves a kind of discomfort, a kind of bad taste,
after it . . . the kind of discomfort one would feel by hearing a line
from Tennyson in the middle of a poem by Robert Burns . . . or a
translation of a line from Tennyson in the middle of a poem in Irish
["fágann sí míchompord éigin, mí-bhlas éigin, ina diaidh, dar liom:
an saghas míchompoird a thiocfadh ar an té a chloisfeadh líne as Tennyson á rá i gcorplár dáin le Robert Burns . . . no aistriúchán ar líne
as Tennyson á rá i gcorplár dáin Ghaeilge]."[22] Ó Ríordáin's phrase,
according to Ó Tuama, comes from a wholly and deliberately non-

Irish milieu (that of English, maybe even England), but Ó Tuama cautions that

> for any Irish-language poet . . . who would live in the big English-speaking world that surrounds us, and who would respond to it with integrity, it would be by necessity dishonest . . . if its trace was not to be found somewhere in his work. . . . A poet who would repress that world inside himself would in doing so repress much of the poetry inside him at the same time.
>
> [Aon fhile Gaeilge, áfach, a chonódh sa domhan fairsing Béarla atá timpeall orainn, is a bheadh ag freagairt go hionraic dó, níor mhór ná gur mhí-mhacánta an mhaise dó gan an rian seo a bheith in áit éigin ar a chuid oibre. . . . An té a mhúchfadh an saol sin ann féin, ba dhóichí dó roinnt mhaith mhór den fhilíocht ann féin a mhúchadh chomh maith.][23]

English never appears directly in the poem in any form, but it silently exerts its influence on the language like the moon on the tides. Ó Tuama describes the effect of reading "My Mother's Burial" as "akin to reading modern English poetry in Irish translation."[24] But English also has a hidden, thematic role in the substance of the poem. Ó Ríordáin has a number of later poems that deal explicitly with the question of the Irish language and his relationship to it: "A Ghaeilge im'Pheannsa" ("O Irish in My Pen"), "A Theanga Seo Leath-Liom" ("O Language Half-Mine"), and, his best-known poem, "Fill Arís" ("Return Again"), which we shall look at later in this chapter. Even though it mentions neither English nor Irish, we can regard "My Mother's Burial" as the first, most powerful and anguished of these, an artistic credo as well as a poem of mourning, a poem about the burial of his mother but also about his decision, as a writer, to consign English, his mother tongue, to the poetic grave.

Ó Tuama draws a connection between the death of Ó Ríordáin's mother and his coming into his own as a poet. His mother's death, Ó Tuama writes, "seems to have helped him to overcome the linguistic and psychological difficulties which had previously hindered his writing."[25] What these linguistic difficulties are, Ó Tuama does not say. But his idea that the loss described in "My Mother's Burial" is also a poetic liberation corresponds at first sight to a well-known Freudian model of male creativity: the need to symbolically kill the mother in order to be reborn as an artist. As in so many other cases, including Proust and Joyce, the painful loss of the mother is also symbolically the beginning of the poet's creative life and artistic identity. In the case of Ó Ríordáin this common "matricidal" idea of male literary endeavor has a more immediate and urgent quality, however, because his poetic life involves abandoning the mother's language and adopting that of the father. The consigning of the mother and her language to the grave is the start of his new, independent artistic life—the mother is silenced so that the artistic voice of the son can speak.

"My Mother's Burial," a poem about a failed attempt at mourning, is about a literal death but also about another one, the white martyrdom of the painful language choice necessary for Ó Ríordáin's poetic vision. If the poem is a farewell to the comforts of maternal love, a farewell yielding the consequent possibility of rebirth as an artist—a familiar enough poetic theme—it is also a farewell to the comforts of writing in one's native, widely spoken language, and to the possibilities of transforming the ordinary words of lived, human interaction into poetry.[26] Since English is his own native language, as Ó Ríordáin parts forever with the security and warmth of maternal love, he is also bidding a painful farewell to the ease and comfort and company of his mother tongue. As the body goes into the grave, with it goes a unique, biological bond of unconditional love, and also the possibility, in his poetry, of embodied, immanent language.

Without ever mentioning English or Irish, the poem provocatively plays with the unspoken paradox of the language it is in, drawing our attention to it in subtle ways. For example:

> I reading a dirtied old letter,
> With every worddrop I drank
> A furious pain piercing my breast,
> Every one of those words squeezed out its own tear.

I remembered the hand that did the writing,

[Seanalitir shalaithe á léamh agam,
Le gach focaldeoch dár ólas
Pian bhinibeach ag dealgadh mo chléibhse,
Do bhrúigh amach gach focal díobh a dheoir féin.

Do chuimhníos ar an láimh a dhein an scríbhinn.]

In these lines, it is the mother's words—not their content but their material, concrete presence—that are the focus of the poet's grief. Ó Coileáin tells us that the letter referred to here is "without doubt" the one written by his mother to him in a sanatorium on March 4, 1944.[27] We do not need to resort to this kind of biographical herme-neutic, however, to detect the phantom of English in these lines. Even if we do not know that Ó Ríordáin's own mother in "real life" spoke only English, we can sense or suspect the material presence of English in the poem in the letter written by her that the poet is clutching at the graveside. The letter is the remainder of English in the poem, the last sign of a now literally unspeakable presence, a lost wholeness. Irish—and the poem—is the sign of its absence.

"My Mother's Burial" shows how the Irish language is bound up for Ó Ríordáin with the creative potential unleashed by death, and other personal and linguistic deaths are layered within the poem. If we read "My Mother's Burial" as a poem that sees the comforts of English and maternal love consigned to the grave together, then we might also go a step further and understand it as a mute revisiting and rewriting by Ó Ríordáin of other earlier, unspoken burials: that of his father, and by extension of the native Irish that he and others took with them. The double death of the mother and, for the poet, of her language, allows for the birth of the poet's creative voice; with the grief attending their loss comes another, hidden, hopeful longing within the martyrdom—to reverse these earlier losses, to resurrect the ghost of his father and his language, to become conjoined with his lost Irish-speaking world.

If the mother's English words are present but muted in the poem, "My Mother's Burial" also deals with the converse question beneath this of the earlier muted parental language, that of the father's Irish. English is the language present but invisible in Ó Ríordáin's poetic world, while Irish was the unspoken presence in his childhood home, a silence that was sealed by the father's early death. In "My Mother's Burial," where the poem explicitly mourns the mother and English, it is also mourning, implicitly, the father and his Irish.

At one moment in the poem, the poet turns from the black hole of his mother's grave to the snow-covered ground, allowing the whiteness to send his mind, by association, away from contemplating her death to imagining her as a young girl in her Communion dress, or as a source of maternal milk:[28]

> And in the midst of the dumbwhite around me
> The darkhole screamed out loud.
>
> The white of a young girl on the day of her First Communion
> The white of the host on the altar on a Sunday
> The white of milk trickling from the breasts
> When they buried my mother, the white of the ground.
>
> [Is i lár na balbh-bháine i mo thimpeall
> Do liúigh os ard sa tsneachta an dúpholl,
>
> Gile gearrachaile lá a céad chomaoine,
> Gile abhlainne Dé Domhnaigh ar altóir,
> Gile bainne ag sreangtheitheadh as na cíochaibh,
> Nuair a chuireadar mo mháthair, gile an fhóid.

But thinking of the mother is also a way to skirt around another, unspeakable black hole and grave. We know that Ó Ríordáin's passionate fascination for native Irish was tied up with his curiosity about his father's life and childhood. The evocation of the mother as a child, the part of her experience her son could never know or share, memories within her that he can never access as she does, is an expression of the ultimate separation of death. But given that the poem is in Irish, the lines can also be read as referring obliquely, perhaps unconsciously, to the Irish-speaking childhood of Ó Ríordáin's father, and by extension again to the lost world of living, embodied Irish.

The white martyrdom of early Irish Christianity consisted not of emigration to a new home but rather of a repudiation of the possibility of home at all, the deliberate choice of exile, of missing, as a mode of living. For Ó Ríordáin, choosing to write in Irish was not a way of finding Irish but a way of missing Irish, even of missing both English and Irish at the same time. Just as Friulian offered Pasolini a way to express the predicament of his sexuality, Irish, the language of the dead and of the spirit, allowed Ó Ríordáin to express the sense of dislocation he felt in the land of the living, and in his own physical body. The language was not a way of going home, as it was for Ó Direáin, but of leaving it, abandoning the condition, the possibility, of home itself. Thus Deleuze and Guattari's condition for a minor literature, that it be "affected with a high coefficient of deterritorialization,"[29] which for them means it must by definition be produced within a major language, applies—in an extreme form—to Ó Ríordáin's Irish. We might, in fact, adapt Deleuze and Guattari's terminology to distinguish between Ó Direáin and Ó Ríordáin: for Ó Direáin, Irish was a wholly, profoundly territorialized language, tied to the rocks and people of Aran. Living in exile in Dublin, his language and his poetic vision are wholly rooted in the landscape and population of his native island (idealized though they may be in his mind). For Ó Ríordáin, Irish is a radically deterritorialized form of language and expression, which has no logically conceivable audience, and no concrete "home" in the real world, no relationship to living speakers of the language, a language within which he is a stranger. We can read "My Mother's Burial" as lamenting this homelessness, for "deterritoralization," a dramatization of the loss (or abandonment) of the comforts of a language that is rooted in a physical people and communities.

Disembodied Irish

This idea illuminates the dramatic critical reception Ó Ríordáin received. The publication of *Eireaball Spideoige* sparked a series of long and heated exchanges in Irish-language journals, literary reviews, and ultimately the columns and book pages of the *Irish Times*. The ferocity of those debates and the intensity of the feelings provoked on both sides by Ó Ríordáin's poetic experiment are difficult to fathom today, and impossible to imagine outside the context of an embattled language. The passions aroused are partly due to the fact that the fear or hope of a revival of the Irish language still had an immediacy in the 1950s that has long since faded. But the sense of high stakes that runs through the debate also reflects an unconscious unease about the increasing sense of Irish—a language whose value as a symbol of unique national identity, after all, was its geographical specificity—as a language cut loose from any physical territory.

It is no surprise that a figure like Ó Ríordáin should have been the focus of controversy: it is the reaction we would expect of a small, aesthetically conservative artistic community to unexpected innovation, such as we would expect to greet the writing of any literary mold breaker. But in the case of Irish-language literature, the question of mold breaking was all the more sensitive because the molds themselves had barely survived: after such a lengthy interruption to high literary endeavor in the language, what was at issue was nothing less than the creation of a future for the language, something that for many was essential to the creation of a future for the nation and the state.

The debate about *Eireaball Spideoige* took a highly unusual form. It tells us less about aesthetics or poetics than it does about the nature of the imaginative investments that had been placed in the language, less about what the poetry meant and more about the hopes, longings, and fears excited by Irish, by its decline and attempted revival. Contrary to what one might expect, few called Ó Ríordáin a charlatan or his work decadent, and his bona fides as a poet, or at least as a potential poet, was rarely questioned. In the *Irish Times*, "Thersites" (the pseudonym of a civil servant called Thomas Woods) praised Ó Ríordáin's talents as a poet but wondered, since Ó Ríordáin was not a native speaker of Irish, whether his work could be considered authentic poetry:

[Ó Ríordáin] has an interesting and sensitive mind, and possesses remarkable skill in rendering his poetic thought into a language of which he is not a native speaker. This should be enough to guarantee that his first book is valuable, though difficult, reading. Yet, I confess to a little doubt in my mind. There can be no doubt of Mr. Ó Ríordáin's quality as a poet, in the abstract. But has he chosen the best channel for communicating? It must be extraordinarily difficult to write poetry in a language that is not native to one (in fact, I suspect that it has never been done). But the problem seems to me almost insoluble, if to this you add the difficulty of your audience. For to whom are Mr. Ó Ríordáin's poems addressed? Hardly to native speakers, who would find difficulty in appreciating fully their import—not only from differences of environment (Mr. Ó Ríordáin is a city dweller), but also because, no matter how excellent Mr. Ó Ríordáin's command of the language is, it can never comprehend that instinctive feel for the connotations of words and phrases that only a native speaker can have. It is possible for classical dons to write Latin and Greek verse, grammatically and metrically beyond reproach and of considerable charm for modern readers; but these verses would indubitably have seemed rather meaningless and possibly absurd to an ancient Roman or Greek. Mr. Ó Ríordáin's audience is rather like that of the classical dons: it is people like myself, who have acquired Irish in school and at college, and the communication involved must necessarily be somewhat artificial. In other words, it is difficult to avoid the impression that what is going on is a highly ingenious but academic exercise, which, whatever its charm, has really very little to do with poetry.[30]

The lengthy back-and-forth that followed Thersites's piece centered not on the quality of Ó Ríordáin's work but on the fact of its being written in Irish. In a more immoderate intervention, the poet Patrick Kavanagh weighed in with a polemic declaring his conviction, even though he could not read Irish, that all poetry written in Irish was nothing more than "the doodlings and phrase-making of mediocrities."[31] Kavanagh's broadside against Ó Ríordáin was perhaps really aimed at his longtime adversary and occasional Irish-language poet, Brendan Behan, and among those who came to Ó Ríordáin's defense in the *Irish Times* was, indeed, Behan, who used Samuel Beckett as a point of comparison: "I don't see however that

Sean O Riordain, born in Baile Mhuirne, is not as well entitled
to write in Irish as Samuel Beckett, born in Dublin, is to write in
French."[32]

Despite this and other interventions on his behalf, the critique
upset Ó Ríordáin. In a letter to his editor, Seán Ó hÉigeartaigh,
not published until ten years after the poet's death, Ó Ríordáin said
that he did count a number of native speakers from the Gaeltacht
among his readership, but ruefully conceded that Thersites had a
point:

> What is causing me pain is not that this thing has been said publicly.
> It is that I am afraid there is some truth in it. I have to admit that
> [Irish] is not my native language. . . . This Thersites has brought up
> an important question. . . . In the case of Máirtín Ó Cadhain, the situ-
> ation is straightforward enough. He is a native speaker. He has the
> Gaelic mindset [*aigne Ghaelach*]. . . . Therefore one can proceed and
> investigate his work and figure out what kind of a writer he is, as one
> would do in any natural country. But there are other writers—the non-
> native writers—and it is not certain whether they should be writing
> in Irish at all.
>
> [Ní hé an rud seo do bheith ráite go poiblí atá ag cur tinnis orm. Is
> amhlaidh atá eagla orm go bhfuil roinnt den fhírinne ann. Ní mór
> dom a admháil nach í [an Ghaeilge] mo theanga dúchais. . . . Tá ceist
> tábhachtach tarraicthe anuas ag an Thersites seo. . . . I gcás Máirtín
> Uí Cadhain tá an scéal símplí go leor. Cainteoir dúchais é. Tá an aigne
> Ghaelach aige. . . . Dá bhrí sin is féidir dul ar aghaidh agus a shaothar
> a iniúchadh féachaint cad é an saghas scríbhneóra é mar a dhéanfaí in
> aon tír nádúrtha. Ach tá scríbhneoirí eile ann—na scríbhneoirí neamh-
> dhúchasacha—agus níl sé cinnte an ceart dóibh scríobh i nGaeilge in
> aon chor.][33]

Thersites's attack, and the exchange of letters in English that ensued,
was an abstract discussion of literature and language, and did not
engage with the substance of Ó Ríordáin's work—Ó hÉigeartaigh
indeed tried to comfort Ó Ríordáin by saying that he thought it unlikely that Thersites had the requisite level of Irish to do so (something that inadvertently raised the whole vexed question of who exactly Ó Ríordáin's intended audience might be).

More significant and detailed critiques of Ó Ríordáin's poetry came in a voluminous and at times savage debate that raged in the Irish-language journals. Read from the point of view of today, these debates offer a fascinating glimpse into the cultural atmosphere of Ireland in the 1950s, the role of the Irish language, and the mix of fears and utopian hopes that were projected onto it. Flann Mac an tSaoir (a pseudonym for Tomás Ó Floinn), for example, wrote that as soon as he read the first poems Ó Ríordáin published in the journal *Comhar* in April 1944, he realized that "an important poet had arrived on the scene [thuigeas . . . go raibh file tábhachtach tagtha ar an bhfód]." Although he praised many aspects of Ó Ríordáin's work, he wrote that the poet was "wrestling with a giant: trying to express the basic sources of his thought and feeling in a language which is perhaps not fully his native language [Tá sé ag coraíocht le fathach: ag iarraidh bunfhoinsí a chuid mhachnaimh agus a chuid mhothúcháin a chur in iúl i dteanga ná fuil, b'fhéidir, ina theanga fíordhúchais aige]."[34]

The most significant and comprehensive attacks on *Eireaball Spideoige*, which were to have a permanent effect on Ó Ríordáin and his work—and thus perhaps indirectly on a whole later generation of Irish-language poets—came from fellow poet Máire Mhac an tSaoi, who was to remain the poet's chief antagonist for the rest of his life. Mhac an tSaoi herself was by some lights not strictly speaking a native speaker either, which may have rendered her especially sensitive to the question of authentic Irish. But she had more respectable academic qualifications to her name, had a more confident command of the literary language, and came from an influential political and academic family—her father had fought in the 1916 Rising—who were key figures in the founding of the state and in its government. Moreover, her own childhood exposure to native Irish had occurred during long periods spent in the flourishing *fíorGhaeltacht* of Dún Chaoin, County Kerry, where the Irish spoken was still rich and where the oral literary tradition was still alive; a far cry from the mottled language of the waning Muskerry Gaeltacht where Ó Ríordáin had grown up.[35]

In her review of *Eireaball Spideoige*, Mhac an tSaoi, like Thersites and Flann Mac an tSaoir before her, took care to praise Ó Ríordáin's talents. She hailed him as a potentially important voice in modern poetry, and even compared some lines favorably to Racine, but she declared that, while much of the poetry itself was of a high intellectual caliber, the risk was that Ó Ríordáin was not writing Irish at all[36] but rather a kind of "Esperanto."[37] Ó Ríordáin, in her view, had a deficient command of Irish and a poor understanding of the possibilities of traditional Irish metrical forms. She went on to detail a long list of instances of *Béarlachas* (anglicism) in his syntax, style, and lexicon, along with an inventory of what she said were straightforward mistakes. She stressed that the problem was not one of raw poetic talent but rather one of the poet's relationship to the Irish language. Ó Ríordáin's Irish, she maintained, was not only riddled with errors but sounded like "something a computer would write." Reading some of his lines, she wrote, was like "crunching sand through your teeth [ag fáisceadh ghainmhe trí d'fhiacla]."[38]

While Ó Ríordáin had a capacity for poetry and for poetic thought, poems that might otherwise have been interesting were marred by "misunderstandings of the meanings of words, or, to put it bluntly, plain bad Irish [mí-thuiscint ar bhrí na bhfocal nó, go neamhbhalbh, gnáth-dhrochGhaeilge]."[39] She ended one of her reviews by advising the poet to go to the living Gaeltacht, if it was not too late—as she implicitly felt it might be—to improve the quality of his Irish.

Ó Ríordáin's answer to Mhac an tSaoi's criticisms was acerbic and robust, but her assessment of his command of the language struck home.[40] He later wrote that they had left him "afraid to write even one word of Irish." Ó Tuama defended both the quality of Ó Ríordáin's Irish and his poetic prerogative, indeed obligation, to write in a form of the language that registered the presence and effect of the English-speaking world in which nearly all Irish writers now lived. His Irish was also defended by the native-speaking Ó Direáin, who responded to many of the individual items on Mhac an tSaoi's list of errors, defending some items as acceptable "native" usages and others as a linguistic form of poetic license.

What is most striking about the controversy—which went on for some time—is the extent to which contributors on both sides disregarded the question of poetry, arguing instead over whether individual lexical items or grammatical forms were correct, permissible, or native. It is a discussion hard to imagine nowadays, and simply unimaginable in a major language. Caoimhín Mac Giolla Léith suggests that we regard "the aridity of this debate [as] an inevitable part of the birth pangs of a new poetry."[41] But there are ways in which this peculiar, impassioned controversy is not merely arid or absurd, and in which the model of progress and birth does not really apply to Ó Ríordáin's experimental use of Irish.

The debate, it seems to me, had ultimately less to do with questions of linguistic purity or aesthetic conservatism, and more to do with questions regarding the ontological status of Irish itself. When he was compiling his *Linguistic Atlas and Survey of Irish Dialects* in the early 1950s, Wagner had been able to turn up informants whose mother tongue was or had been Irish in at least twenty out of the thirty-two counties of Ireland, including in places long thought of as thoroughly English-speaking, such as Kilkenny and Cavan. Most of these remaining native speakers of local dialects of Irish from outside the Gaeltacht (often anomalous cases, such as people who had been fostered out to elderly relatives) died in the 1940s and 1950s (the last native speaker of Monaghan Irish came from Kavanagh's own Inniskeen, and died in 1957, for example).[42] With them went the last traces and memory of the time when Irish was a widespread and unremarkable part of daily life right across the island. The forties and fifties were the first decades in which Irish as a naturally spoken language seemed never to have been "general over Ireland" but to belong as a matter of innate identity to the Gaeltacht, the preserve of a handful of specific areas of the country. Outside the Gaeltacht, the last traces of its living memory had now finally faded, and the link to Irish became a notional, abstract, and even somewhat mystical thing. The language was fossilized in place-names, but alien to the people who lived there; it leaked, one might say, out of bodies and into the earth and air.

These were the first decades without a live memory of Irish as a living, breathing, tangible local reality, of something that had been at home, a given, in all parts of Ireland. The country was now divided, in terms of native speech, between an English-speaking area and a handful of cordoned-off Irish-speaking enclaves. To think of the Irish language as a whole linguistic ocean of its own, even a receding one (as one could still think of Welsh or Breton) now required an active work of the imagination, almost an act of faith.

This context sheds some light on the debate around *Eireaball Spideoige*. Mhac an tSaoi's chief objection to Ó Ríordáin's experiments was that they showed a disregard for the fact that Irish was a "living language." A comment of Ó Ríordáin's, in later years, that Mhac an tSaoi's own writing was concerned not with producing poetry but with producing Irish, is on the face of it equally strange, and intended as a quick put-down, but it is telling.[43] The problem which exercised, and indeed seems to have tacitly confused readers on both sides of the disagreement about *Eireaball Spideoige*, was that of how to differentiate between what were simply lexical or syntactical errors made by someone who had not been fully brought up in the language—a "foreigner's" mistakes, as it were—and what could be viewed as modernist experiment and innovation within an existing language framework.[44] This would be an easy distinction to draw in languages such as English, French, and Italian (Vladimir Nabokov and Beckett being cases in point). But for a language that had disappeared as living speech from everywhere but a few scattered communities with little formal culture, the very existence of such a framework could not be taken as a given. The unspoken anxiety underlying the controversy over *Eireaball Spideoige*, in fact, was that the whole concept of a native modern literary language was uneasily close to having the status of a theoretical construct, almost a counterfactual hypothesis (how Irish would now be written if English had not succeeded in supplanting it; Irish written for the kind of reader who would have existed had the battle of Kinsale turned out differently). Ó Ríordáin's innovation, in other words, posed an existential problem for the language itself: the issue animating the controversy over *Eireaball Spideoige* was at heart not about poetry or modernism or literary experiment but about the question of what Irish was, whose it was, or, perhaps most acutely, *where* it was.

Ó Ríordáin's poetic achievement risked bringing the paradoxes inherent in the uncomfortable imbalance between native Irish and learned Irish to a head, a loose thread that threatened to pull apart the fabric of the logic of the language revival. I am not suggesting that any of his critics or admirers consciously thought this way but rather that the emergence of deliberately unexamined fault lines and deliberately unspoken contradictions in the situation—the desire to keep up the necessary fictions of the language movement—lay beneath the fierceness of the reaction to *Eireaball Spideoige*. The underlying motivation was not hostility to literary innovation per se but a sense—a subconscious or at most semiconscious one—that it would reveal the gaps and absences that lay at the secret heart of the dreams they had invested in Irish. The discourse was driven, this is to say, by an unconscious fear not of something but of the revelation of a nothing, or of a nowhere.

The idea of disembodied language is the key modernist quality of post-vernacular Irish-language literature. Ó Ríordáin himself linked his own horror at the inauthenticity of his Irish to his disgust with his own body. A chronic invalid, for whom being a tubercular patient became a crucial aspect of his identity, he frequently links the defectiveness of his body to his awareness of not being a native speaker of Irish: he is at home in neither language nor body. The horror of the body, the sense of being imprisoned within it, of not being at home in it, appears frequently in Ó Ríordáin's writing (especially in his letters from the TB sanatorium, for example, "I hate the naked body [is gráin liom an corp lom]"[45] or "I feel utterly hostile to the palms of my hands. My arse fills me with undying hatred").[46] His disgust with his body is, of course, related to the austere Catholicism of his times, but it is also, more powerfully, related to the question of language choice.

Associating the Irish language with chastity—and thus English with sexual sin—was not uncommon in the Catholic side of the revival.

Patrick Pearse had written of the people of north Connemara: "Only on the lonelier mountain slopes—Binn Ghuaire, Dochruadh, and Cnoc Leitreach—does one find the *ipsissimus* Gael—the Gael as he was in the days when Grainne Mhaol's warships swept these seas, and the clans that garrisoned these mountains were wont periodically to swoop down on the burghers of Galway and Athenry. I met him last week beyond Cnoc Leitreach—met strong men and women in the prime of life whose Irish organs of speech have never been defiled by a word of English."[47] Our examples of Pasolini and Behan suggest that Pearse's projections onto the Irish language were likely bound up with his own (unacknowledged) homosexuality. It is easy to ridicule this rhetoric that nowadays reads like a parody of itself, but what Pearse is praising in this delirious paean to native Irish speakers is analogous to what Pasolini saw in Livio Socolari's Friulian, the natural way in which the language seems to him to reside in their bodies, the ways that Irish and their bodies seem to be at home in one another, native to one another.

Sexuality, bodily sickness, and the language question are connected in analogous ways in the case of Ó Ríordáin. In the passages in his diary and letters where he decries the unnatural, artificial, inhuman quality of his Irish, Ó Ríordáin often refers to his body in the same terms. In the diary entry comparing himself to Ó Direáin, for example, he conflates the sickness of his body, his own moral failings and the nonnativeness of his Irish:

> What was my bad luck the day I decided to go with Irish? I have spent today and yesterday and the day before that here in bed coughing up diseased spit without anyone around me. I am dying. I am deceived, I have deceived myself, I am an object of public mockery. It is said of me that I am an Irish [-language] writer. I have spent my life, my energies on Irish, and I will never have Irish. All I have, and all I ever will have, is this dead thing that I am hawking here. How did I convince so many people? Am I not a fraud? Am I not preaching a creed in which I myself do not believe? What is all this fraudulence for? . . . The truth is something alive. There is truth in Máirtín Ó Direáin's Irish. There is life in it. There is no truth in my Irish nor in me. Nor any life either.

My Irish is as rotten, as diseased as I am. Is there anyone in Ireland as rotten as me, as useless as me? If I recover from this illness, I will go out spreading lies again! Oh, oh, oh, the pain. There is some skill in my Irish, some cleverness. All it is lacking is truth and life.

[Cad é an mí-ádh a bhí orm an chéad lá dul le Gaeilge? Tá an lá inniu agus an lá inné agus an lá roimis sin caite agam anso sa leabaidh ag caitheamh amach seilí galair gan aoinne faram. Táim ag fáil bháis. Táim meallta—meallta agam féin, im cheap magaidh go poiblí. Tá sé amuigh orm gur scríbhneoir Gaeilge mé. Tá mo shaol, mo dhúthracht, caite agam le Gaeilge agus ní bheidh Gaeilge go bráth agam. Níl agam, ná ní bheidh, ach an rud marbh atá á reic agam anso. Conas a mheallas an oiread san daoine? Nach bithiúnach mé? Ná fuilim ag craoladh creidimh ná creidim féin? . . . Rud beo an fhírinne. Tá an fhírinne i nGaeilge Mháirtín Uí Dhireáin. Tá beatha inti. Níl an fhírinne im Ghaeilgese ná ionam féin. Níl ná beatha. Tá mo chuid Gaeilge chomh lofa, chomh galrach liom féin. Bhfuil aoinne in Éirinn chomh lofa liom, chomh neamhthairfeach? Má thagann biseach orm ón mbreoiteacht so, amach ag scaipeadh éithigh a raghad arís! Ó, Ó, Ó, an phian. Tá aiclíocht áirithe, gliocas áirithe, sa Ghaeilge seo agamsa. Níl in easnamh uirthi ach fírinne agus beatha.][48]

This sense of Irish as a language unanchored from bodies was experienced by him as an adult in immediate and straightforward ways. Irish had effectively no natural role as a spoken language in his own personal life. His vehement description, for example, of the mortifying fakeness of two native speakers of English deliberately speaking Irish together in public, points to the hollowness, on an immediate, experiential level, of the language revival in its actualized as opposed to theoretical version, to the gap between the utopian *ideal* of a language and the grubby reality of language in its actual daily instantiation, as a medium of ordinary communication between people, between bodies.

Native speakers like Ó Direáin or Pearse's mountainy Connemara men, or Pasolini's Livio Socolari, appear to the longing gaze of the nonnative poet not to suffer from this division between language and body; the ideal language seems to spring miraculously from them as a natural medium of everyday life and human fellowship. There is a visceral, physical quality to Ó Ríordáin's description of the falseness of trying to speak Irish with fellow *Gaeilgeoirí*, to whom spontaneous social communication would come naturally in English. Irish is an ideal language that withers into unreality at any attempt to realize it in real time, bodies, and space. Ó Ríordáin bemoans the social awkwardness of using Irish with other mother-tongue English enthusiasts, Dineen's "stammerers," but in poetic terms, this is the value of Irish for him: it allows him to experience, in an immediate, physical way, the gap between the quotidian and the eternal, between the individual and the collective, the body and the soul. Irish, the nonnative language in which he longs to be native, as his father was, renders visible the holes and absences in language itself, the full size of the gulf between ourselves and others that language is supposed to bridge; in adopting a language with no place, in fleeing embodied language, Ó Ríordáin entered a linguistic reality in which all the wounds and failures of language, its alienness and fundamentally inhospitable nature, could be keenly felt.

Ó Ríordáin does not reflect openly on how the emotional terrain of his childhood attachments to his parents and their languages might be bound up in the unforgiving linguistic martyrdom he chose for himself.[49] But in a 1958 essay defending his poetic practice and outlining his philosophy of language, he comes close to articulating a vision of Irish as a utopian reality always just out of reach and out of sight. "Teangacha Príobháideacha" ("Private Languages") was broadcast on national radio and subsequently published in installments in the Irish-language newspaper *Inniu*. As Mac Giolla Léith points out, "Private Languages" was in essence a defense of the poetic practice of *Eireaball Spideoige*,[50] and the essay includes some well-aimed potshots at Mhac an tSaoi. But it also touches, almost inadvertently, on deeper, more revealing issues, especially in its reflection on the relationship between language and dialect and between ideal and actualized language.

For Mac Giolla Léith, the most telling point of the essay is Ó Ríordáin's "insistence on the writer's ability to create from his or her linguistic inheritance a 'brand new, wholly native language.'"[51]

Ó Ríordáin's theory of a writer forging a private language is a hopeful response to his own fears and insecurities about the meaning of his creative work in Irish. In the essay he puts forward a range of interesting examples of writers, such as St. John of the Cross, who, in his view, forged their own "private languages." But more interesting for our purposes is the way he goes on to imagine that all of the different varieties in which a given language is used are partial, incomplete manifestations of a whole, complete, but in itself inaccessible, linguistic soul. Ó Ríordáin never says it outright, but it seems to me that he is hinting at the idea, which we encountered in Joyce's "The Dead," that everyone is a foreigner to the language he or she speaks. In discussing whether or not the Irish language per se can be said to exist (a rhetorical question that, as I have been arguing, is the unspoken anxiety underlying modern Irish-language literature and the discourse surrounding it), he writes: "An underlying framework may be perceived behind all the dialects [of Irish] and they reveal a distinctive spirit [*meanma*]. There is no idiom in any dialect that does not conform to this underlying framework and spirit. . . . Every writer, therefore, who is familiar with any one of the dialects has an image of the Irish language in his mind. And the fact that this image is in his mind enables him to create a brand new, wholly native language from the speech of his ancestors" (translation by Mac Giolla Léith).[52]

Mac Giolla Léith points out that here that Ó Ríordáin's idea comes close to an independent formulation of Saussure's distinction between *langue* and *parole*. In theory, Ó Ríordáin is using Irish merely as an example of something that would apply to any language, but his theory inadvertently addresses the taboo question of deterritorialized Irish, of what or where Irish is, once the living language of the Gaeltacht has shrunk almost out of sight. Ó Ríordáin's choice of words is revealing, whether consciously or otherwise: the "private language" that the writer can create for himself from the speech of his ancestors is, he writes, *lándúchasach*, "wholly native"; this word could not be more loaded for Ó Ríordáin, criticized for, and tormented by, but perhaps finally inspired by, the nonnativeness of his own command of Irish. *Dúchasach* means "native," as in native speaker, but also as in native to a place; *lándúchasach*, "wholly native" is precisely what Ó Ríordáin can never be in Irish, which is for him a state of homelessness, a state of longing to finally come home to the *meanma* of the language, a true linguistic home that can always be sensed but never seen or arrived at, a sense of wholeness and plenitude in which self, place, and language would be a single, whole, organically interconnected reality, a perfect ecosystem.

Ó Ríordáin's platonic account of language in the essay suggests that the homeland of Irish is a place that can be intuited or imagined but never inhabited. The essay, difficult as it is to follow, is in the end an acknowledgment, an unconscious one it seems, that the nativeness and truth Ó Ríordáin is seeking in Irish are not really of this world, a powerful presence in the terrain of the imagination but not locatable on a map or in a body. In Ó Ríordáin's account in "Private Languages," any actualized form of Irish, any utterance issuing from a real place or from a physical body, is merely a signpost to an elsewhere of linguistic plenitude, a place of true nativeness, of being fully at home in language. We can perceive the existence of this world and something of its nature through these manifestations, but it in itself remains mysterious and inaccessible, always "next door."

Croce's distinction between "spontaneous" and "reflected" use of dialect (see chapter 2) is of surprising salience in Ireland, where the difference between the two is as constitutive of modern Irish-language writing as it is taboo to mention. The literary use of Irish can clearly be divided into spontaneous and reflected use, but the poetic nature of the choice has been elided by the national question of language revivalism. Croce's binary is particularly helpful as a description of modern literary Irish, where "spontaneous" use of Irish is found in the ever-shrinking vernacular Gaeltacht tradition, and where reflected use, covering all of those who write in Irish as a second language, or even anyone who writes in a form of Irish intended for a non-Gaeltacht audience, dominates. The distinction between speaking Irish spontaneously and choosing to use Irish for particular reasons is essential to Ó Ríordáin's work.

In Italy, unlike in Ireland, most educated people were used to switching between the major and the minor language for different purposes, but dialect was always bound up with place and context. Croce's idea was quite different: that writing in dialect did not have to be tied to its spoken life in the community, only to the individual poet's internal vision. Writing in dialect, he wrote, did not have to be an "exact, historical reproduction of the life and character of the people whose dialect [the writer] is employing [esatto e storico riproduttore della vita e del carattere di quel popolo di cui adopera il dialetto]"; nor did it even have to follow any established version of the spoken dialect, so long as it corresponded to [the poet's] personal vision.[53] From Croce's ideas onward, according to Brevini, twentieth-century literature in dialect continued along a path of "ever-increasing divergence between dialect and its referents [sulla strada di una crescente divarcazione del dialetto dei suoi referenti]."[54] Croce's reflections would be almost heretical in the Irish context, in which the revival of the language had to be understood as the prime motivator behind even the most abstruse literary enterprise; but, perhaps partly because of this, they are enormously illuminating about the creative use of Irish and the debates that surrounded it. Croce was writing this essay[55] at the height of the "speech of the people" movement in Ireland, which took the language of Irish-speaking communities as a literary model, and their lived experience as the proper matter for writing. Croce's modernist reframing of dialect as a self-consciously chosen literary medium reads almost like a defense of Ó Ríordáin's poetic practice twenty years later, an answer to the criticisms that he was ignoring the living language and writing in a kind of Esperanto. A voice like Croce's that would change the very terms in which the choice of the Irish language as a literary medium was understood was impossible in newly independent Ireland, where the question of language use could not be separated from that of language, and hence national, loyalty. Ó Ríordáin himself, a dyed-in-the-wool nationalist and revivalist, would never have defended his own work on Croce's grounds. He never publicly eschewed the speech of the people as a poetic ideal or Irish as a national goal but, despite himself, continued to produce poetry in a form of the language that was neither local nor national but artificial and highly individual.

Applying Croce's idea of the "reflected" use of dialect to Ó Ríordáin's use of Irish allows us to revisit Mhac an tSaoi's assessment of Ó Ríordáin's idiosyncratic form of Irish as "Esperanto." Mhac an tSaoi chose the word as a dismissive criticism of what she felt was the inhuman, rootless feeling of his diction—a betrayal, as she saw it, of the living, spoken, territorialized language. Those who defended Ó Ríordáin's Irish at the time did so on the basis that she was wrong, that his Irish was, in fact, native and grounded. But we might defend it on different terms. Esperanto is a language deliberately designed not to be tethered to one place or people; it is a utopian language in both the literal, etymological sense that it is placeless, the language of a no-place, but also in the sense that it comes out of a desire for a new way of living and communicating in the world (the word, after all, means "hope").

Return Again

"Oíche Nollaig na mBan" ("The Night [i.e., eve] of Women's Christmas"), one of Ó Ríordáin's best known and most anthologized poems, is on the face of it about passing from life to death. It is a characteristically bleak poem in which the poet imagines himself dying alone at home on the eve of the Feast of the Epiphany, the same day of the year that Joyce's "The Dead" takes place (traditionally known in Ireland as "Women's Christmas," *Nollaig na mBan*), listening to the wailing and screeching of life outside in order not to notice himself slipping into death. In the poem, the poet imagines himself returning home from a dance and waiting in the darkness for death to come. In its structural division between the solitude of the poet's house and the rest of the world, we might discern traces of Ó Ríordáin's divided life between lonely poetic endeavor in Irish in Inniscarra and family, work, and social life in English in Cork.

The poet imagines that he would like death to come to him when he is "Returning home from the dance of life / As the light of sin goes out [Ag filleadh abhaile ó rince an tsaoil / Is solas an pheaca ag dul as]." "Returning home" is what the poet will exhort himself and others to do by turning to the Irish language in his most famous poem "Fill Arís" ("Return Again"), in which the poet urges the reader, or himself, to return to his "true shape [cló ceart]." In Irish *saol*, "life," also means the world, and especially the social world (something like *monde* in French). The phrase "rince an tsaoil," "the dance of life," therefore has a double resonance, life itself, what the poet will have to abandon when he dies, but also the chattering world of other people, the "dance" of social interactions and concerns that he leaves behind when he returns home. It is life and death for sure, but it is also English and Irish, the "dance" of intimacy and intercourse with other people, frivolous and even insane, versus the stasis, isolation, silence, and bodiless purity of the poet's home. In the Ireland of the 1940s and 1950s, moreover, when the poem was written, the word "dance" had a connotation of occasions for sexual sin, events at which young couples got together and which were heavily policed and often closed down by priests. Indeed the word *saol*, which used to be spelled *saoghal*, is etymologically linked to *saeculum*, and thus to "secular," in all its connotations of the mortal but also irreligious world. This meaning of the phrase "the dance of life" is reinforced by the otherwise mysterious next line when the poet refers to dying as "the light of sin going out [solas an pheaca ag dul as]": sin, sexuality, and social life are bound up with English and vernacular life, and bodiless purity with Irish and poetry and truth. (English is explicitly construed in one of Ó Ríordáin's poems as a sexual temptress, a "foreign harlot," "striapach allúrach.")

The same connection is present in a poem by Michael Hartnett, much later in the twentieth century, "Farewell to English," in which the poet announces his decision to write henceforth only in Irish as an act of solidarity with the last of the Gaelic bards, adrift in a violently altered linguistic landscape:

> But I will not see
> great men go down
> who walked in rags
> from town to town
> finding English a necessary sin,
> the perfect language to sell pigs in.[56]

In this poem, for Hartnett, as for Ó Ríordáin, English is the language of materialism and sin, and Irish that of authentic thought and feeling, but also, by implication, solitude. In the most immediate sense, Hartnett is referring to the language of the marketplace in opposition to that of art and spirit, but the word "sin," repeated in the "pigs in" rhyme, also has the sense of bodily sin, first in the meaning of sexual sin but also, by extension, the "sin," or "dance," of quotidian human interactions, with all their imperfections, seams, and inadequacies. English is associated here with fallenness and secularism, with commerce or intercourse, in a variety of overlapping senses, economic, social, sexual, emotional.

This distinction clearly held for Pasolini in how he conceived of *lingua* and *dialetto*. One of his poems in which he addresses Friuli itself bears directly upon Hartnett's poem here and upon Ó Ríordáin's conceit of his sullying Irish with what he picked up from a "foreign harlot":

> You cannot forgive, O Christian Friuli,
> one who freed your enslaved tongue
> in a heart warm with sin.
>
> [No ti pos perdonàighi tu, Friùl
> cristiàn, a un che la to lenga sclava
> ta un còur cialt di peciàt al dispeava.] (I.100)

Unlike Pasolini with Friuli, Ó Ríordáin did not construe Dún Chaoin as a sexual paradise, still less as a homosexual one, but the imaginary realm of Irish to which he longs to escape is subtly construed in his poetry as a place that is free from the other great preoccupation of mid-twentieth-century Ireland, sexual sin. To leave English for Irish is to abandon sin but also to abandon "the dance of life." The "light of sin" that goes out in "The Night of Women's Christmas" can be understood as the bodily pleasures offered by the "harlot" of English, not disconnected by any means from the bodily comforts of his mother and her English to which the poet bids a pained farewell in "My Mother's Burial"; indeed, the title "The Night of Women's Christmas" may even hint that to abandon English for Irish is to abandon the world of women altogether (as in Pasolini's "The Dead Boy," with the poet turning away from the pregnant woman to Narcissus staring at himself in the pool, also suggests). From his childhood Irish was for Ó Ríordáin the language of those dead, absent, or next door, English the language of living bodies, presence, the here and now. "The Night of Women's Christmas" is implicitly a poem about what it would really be like to succeed in returning "home" to Irish—beyond the pleasure principle, free from body, sin, thus pure, bodiless, and at rest.

Even if it is registered as a death wish in "The Night of Women's Christmas," the longing to really go native, to seek out and find a living world of Irish was a real and urgent one for Ó Ríordáin. Despite the gloom and bitterness of his own views of his command of Irish, the desperate longing associated with his devotion to the language is a genuine desire, a real utopian impulse. In "Private Languages" he seems on one level to tacitly register the "deterritorialized" nature of his Irish and its centrality to his poetic practice. But, just as Pasolini sought to realize his utopian idea of Friulian in real people and places, Ó Ríordáin did engage in a serious attempt to close the gap between body and spirit, and to remap Irish onto a specific geographical territory and community. In the early 1950s, dissatisfied with what he felt was the poor quality of his Ballyvourney Irish, and stung by the criticisms he had received, Ó Ríordáin began spending long periods in the west Kerry parish of Dún Chaoin, across the water from the Blasket Islands, which had seen such a flowering of native literary Gaelic in the 1920s and 1930s. Unlike Baile Bhuirne, Irish was not dying in Dún Chaoin, and in the 1950s it was the undisputed, vibrant vernacular of the community, old and young. Dún Chaoin was—and is—the last bastion of native Munster Irish, the dialect closest to the old high literary standard.[57] The people of the area were renowned for their instinctive and rich command of the language and for their knowledge of the ancient oral repertoire.

The title of *Eireaball Spideoige* ("A Robin's Tail") was taken from "My Mother's Burial," and it announces the beginning of Ó Ríordáin's linguistic martyrdom, the relegation of his mother, his mother tongue, and the comforts of embodied presence to the grave. His second collection, *Brosna* ("Kindling"), published in 1964, twelve years after *Eireaball Spideoige*,[58] ends with "Fill Arís," "Return Again," a poem that supposedly announces the poet's discovery, at last, of the previously undreamt-of linguistic potential of Dún Chaoin, the discovery of embodied Irish.

"Return Again" rewrites "My Mother's Burial" by mapping the poet's artistic journey from English to Irish not in psychological but in explicit, and indeed quite specific, geographical terms—not merely Ireland, or Kerry, but the single parish of Dún Chaoin. "Return Again" is an account of the poetic-political program behind Ó Ríordáin's decision to write in Irish, but also a lyric expression of the inner longings that drove this decision. Séamus Heaney saw this double duty in the poem when he wrote that "as well as being a polemic ["Return Again] is an expression of the writer's inner division, and of his repining for that universal, paradisiacal place where our conflicts will be resolved."[59]

What these conflicts are, Heaney does not say. The poem is a nationalist as well as lyric project, an exhortation to reconnect to the past and to a native tradition, to move from an imposed, unnatural, and sullied inheritance—the "halter" of English—to a birthright, to a language as natural as the evening sunshine or the cliffs. The poem is widely admired. Heaney was captivated by it (it seems to me that he revisits "Return Again," many years later, in his own poem "Postscript," which begins: "And some time make the time to drive out west"). Ó Tuama thought it a "graceful" poem, Ó Ríordáin's most accomplished. But its content is criticized even by these admirers as a narrow-minded, chauvinistic, and naïve project. Ó Tuama writes that in it Ó Ríordáin "argues—rather improbably—that his real self can only be realized in the Kerry Gaeltacht when he has shaken off the crippling effect of English civility, of Shelley, Keats and Shakespeare."[60] Heaney wrote that "the poem, in its sectarian application, would refuse to recognize history and language other than its own espoused versions of them."[61]

While "Return Again" may be, on one level, about Ó Ríordáin's decision to spend time in Dún Chaoin and embrace the living language, a poem explicitly about reterritorializing the dream of Irish to a real place and real people,[62] the poem bears rereading in the light of Croce and Pasolini.

> *Return Again*
> Leave Gleann na nGealt [the Valley of the Mad] back east,
> And all there is of this age of our Lord in your blood
> Close your mind to what has happened
> Since the Battle of Kinsale,
> And, since the load is heavy
> And the road long, remove from your mind
> The civilized halter of English,
> Shelley, Keats and Shakespeare:
> Return again to your own,
> Cleanse your mind and cleanse
> Your tongue which got tied up in a syntax
> At odds with your intellect:
> Make your confession and make
> Peace with your own race,
> And with your own house and do not abandon them.
> It is not natural for anyone to abandon his house or his tribe.
> On a sunlit evening take the cliff road out to Corca Dhuibhne,
> And out on the horizon you will see shoaling there
> The Dual Number, and the Subjunctive Mood
> And the vocative case on people's mouths:
>
> That is your door,
> Dún Chaoin in the evening light
> Knock and there will be opened to you
> Your own mind and your right shape.

[*Fill Arís*

Fág Gleann na nGealt thoir,
Is a bhfuil d'aois seo ár dTiarna i d'fhuil,
Dún d'intinn ar ar tharla
Ó buaileadh Cath Chionn tSáile,
Is ón uair go bhfuil an t-ualach trom
Is an bóthar fada, bain ded mheabhair
Srathar shibhialtacht an Bhéarla,
Shelley, Keats is Shakespeare:
Fill arís ar do chuid,
Nigh d'intinn is nigh
Do theanga a chuaigh ceangailte i gcomhréiribh
'Bhí bunoscionn le d'éirim:
Dein d'fhaoistin is dein
Síocháin led ghiniúin féinig
Is led thigh-se féin is ná tréig iad,
Ní dual do neach a thigh ná a threibh a thréigean.
Téir faobhar na faille siar tráthnóna gréine go Corca Dhuibhne,
Is chífir thiar ag bun na spéire ag ráthaíocht ann
An Uimhir Dhé, is an Modh Foshuiteach,
Is an tuiseal gairmeach ar bhéalaibh daoine:

Sin é do dhoras,
Dún Chaoin fé sholas an tráthnóna,
Buail is osclófar
D'intinn féin is do chló ceart.][63]

The poem is built around an east-west axis ("Leave the Valley of
the Mad back east"—"Go west along the cliff road [Fág Gleann na
nGealt thoir—Téir faobhar na faille siar]"). In going from east to
west, the poet is retracing the historical trajectory of the decline of
the Irish language in the country, to its last refuge here at the edge
of the Atlantic peninsula of Corca Dhuibhne. The movement also
corresponds to the journey "home from the dance of life" in "The
Night of Women's Christmas," to Ó Ríordáin's childhood movement
between his own family home and the houses of his Irish-speaking
neighbors, and to the adult division he created between his social and
economic life in English in Cork city and his solitary Gaelic refuge

in Inniscarra. But the east-west division of the poem also refers, in the wake of the reception of *Eireaball Spideoige*, to the distinction between learned Irish and native Irish. It announces Ó Ríordáin's discovery, at last, of the riches of the vernacular Irish spoken by the people of Dún Chaoin and his supposed determination to go there to renew his command of the language and in so doing renew himself and his soul.

The process of moving west to native Irish is expressed in terms of religious purification: "Cleanse your mind and cleanse / Your tongue," "Make your confession and make / Peace with your own race," "It is not natural for anyone to abandon his house or his tribe," "Your proper [i.e., right, good] shape." As the poet moves out of English-speaking Ireland and into the Gaeltacht, he is cleansed of sin. The idea of the poem seems to be that in achieving this state the poet would be going home, and the line "It is not natural for anyone to leave his home or his tribe [Ní dual do neach a thigh ná a threibh a thréigean]" seems to suggest just that. But the movement between one home and another was fundamental in Ó Ríordáin's linguistic biography, and we know that to embrace Irish, as the poem urges us to do, he had to abandon the language of the home in which he grew up. The line, in the context of Ó Ríordáin's childhood, can be read as meaning exactly the reverse of what it first implies, not returning to the home of Irish, but leaving the home of English in search of Irish in the world beyond it.

Moving to the Gaeltacht will not simply purify his Irish (as Mhac an tSaoi recommended) but also purify his soul. This disembodied, spiritual idea is described, however, in highly specific geographical terms. Gleann na nGealt, literally "Valley of the Mad," refers to a real place on the Dingle Peninsula, the last English-speaking village before one crosses into the Gaeltacht; it is the place where, when going to Dún Chaoin, in Ó Ríordáin's worldview, one passes out of the materialist desert of English and into the poetic paradise of Irish.[64] In these last stanzas, the poem appears to be attempting to reterritorialize its dreams, mapping the longed-for true home onto the natural landscape of Corca Dhuibhne.

This attempt finds itself in conflict, however, with the insistently incorporeal quality of what the poet is actually promised to find there: shoaling subjunctives and doors that creak open of their own accord. The poem flickers between Dún Chaoin as a *paese dell'anima*, landscape of the soul, and that of a real place. This complex set of connections between sin, sexuality, purity, and language have obvious resonances with Pasolini's imaginative construction of a world where homosexuality would be unmarked, and thus sinless—in the Friulian language—and with the final clash between this ideal and bodily reality in the sexual scandal that ended his Friulian experiment. In "Return Again" the two realms, the inner poetic vision and the external geographical, human place, finally converge in the last lines. If one were actually to follow the directions in the poem and travel across the Dingle Peninsula as far west as it is possible to go, and stop at the Atlantic Ocean in Dún Chaoin and look across the horizon, where the poet sees abstract grammatical forms and a door, one would, in "real life," so to speak, see the Blasket Islands, a few miles across the sound. According to the map he gives us, the poet must be looking directly at the looming shape of the Great Blasket, five miles offshore from Dún Chaoin.

As evidenced by Behan's poem, the Blaskets were of immense importance for modern Irish-language literature. Their Irish-speaking peasant population became a focus of intense interest for British and Scandinavian anthropologists in the late nineteenth and early twentieth centuries who recorded the islanders' ancient way of life and rich repertoire of oral culture. The result was a spate of extraordinary memoirs published in the 1920s, most notably *An tOileánach* (*The Islandman*) by Tomás Ó Criomhthain in 1929, *Fiche Bliain ag Fás* (*Twenty Years A-Growing*) by Muiris Ó Súilleabháin in 1933, and *Peig* by Peig Sayers in 1936. For the Irish-language literary world their effect was huge. The authors of these memoirs had had little formal education but did have a sophisticated command of the language and a dizzying array of mythological and folkloric material at their disposal. They quickly became the very symbol of the almost mystical properties attributed to the living language, the embodiment of spontaneous native genius and of the natural—as opposed to artificial—transmission of the Gaelic tradition. Their language became the gold standard of the rare combination of literary and native; Ó Ríordáin, who met her, wrote that his own Irish was "thin" compared with that of Peig Sayers. But since the Blaskets represented a way of life and a cultural world that had vanished from the rest of Ireland (and Europe), they also stood for all that was being lost, for good, as naturally Irish-speaking Ireland disappeared.

The Great Blasket had had a sizable population during the years of the Famine, but poverty and emigration whittled this down to an unsustainable handful of largely elderly people, and the islands were evacuated by government order in 1953, the year in which *Eireaball Spideoige* was published, with the remaining islanders resettled on the mainland in Dún Chaoin. When Ó Ríordáin wrote "Return Again," the Blaskets had been unpopulated for some years. In these famous lines, usually considered to be a triumphal, if deluded, account of the poet finding his spiritual home on earth in the Kerry Gaeltacht, the poet, as he looks for his linguistic utopia, is actually looking at the abandoned Blaskets. The supposed reterritorialization involved in discovering Dún Chaoin quietly cedes to the disembodied nature of what the language promises. Just as in Behan's poem "Jackeen ag Caoineadh na mBlascaod" ("A Jackeen Lamenting the Blaskets"), depicting the splendors and sounds of nature on the Blaskets with no human life there to witness them, in "Return Again," when the poet makes his pilgrimage westward, what he finds is not an ideal community of people but language as pure, disembodied form—"the Dual Number, and the Subjunctive Mood, / And the vocative case"—and islands (the unnamed Blaskets) with nobody living on them.

In the idealized languages that Pasolini and Ó Ríordáin chose for their poetry, each sought a dream of a purer, incorruptible form of connection to the self, to others and to the world, the possibility of intercourse of all kinds in a state of grace, a place of pure abstract forms, without bodies, and thus without sin. The same paradox characterized Ó Ríordáin's choice of Irish and Pasolini's of Friulian: the idea that by setting themselves *at odds* with language, by "going nonnative," they will access this impossible, purified kind of nativeness; only by going nonnative can the impossible dream of full nativeness be perceived. It was the partial, half-dead nature of the modern Irish language as Ó Ríordáin encountered it that allowed for the articulation of a utopian vision of linguistic plenitude and life not available in the fallen, vernacular, embodied world of the living.

What is involved is not a completed journey, but an impossible trajectory. In the final revelatory, hallucinatory lines of "Return Again," the poet does appear to arrive at a natural paradise: "Dún Chaoin in the evening light," "Dún Chaoin faoi sholas an tráthnóna." We seem to have moved from "the silk of the afternoon," "síoda an tráthnóna," in "My Mother's Burial" to "the light of the afternoon," "solas an tráthnóna," from something man-made to the natural world. When, however, he arrives at his destination and looks at his promised land on the horizon, what he sees is not a vision of physical nature but abstract, obscure grammatical forms, invented categories of language used only by outsiders and learners, not by natives, an emblematic instance of "reflected use":

> And out on the horizon you will see shoaling there
> The Dual Number, and the Subjunctive Mood
> And the vocative case on people's mouths.

For Pasolini, it was the natural, unconscious connection between the voice, tongue, and lips of Livio Socolari and the words that he uttered that attracted him to Friulian, but also underscored his insurmountable apartness from it. If you can see it, you cannot be it. Here, in Ó Ríordáin's narrative of the poet's pilgrimage to the Gaeltacht to improve his Irish and absorb the spirit of the living language, this vision of grammatical forms is a stark expression, as for the gay Pasolini in Friuli, of his nonnativeness. For native speakers, grammatical forms are invisible, undifferentiated parts of the natural order of the world; for them, to speak Irish (or Friulian) is just to speak. But they are highly visible to the poet, shoaling on the horizon, on the mouths of other people, across the water from him.

The vision here of the distant, promised land shimmering on the horizon across from Dún Chaoin—at once the unnamed, unpopulated Blaskets and the disembodied forms and structures of the Irish language—is confused with the legend of Hy-Brasil, Tír na nÓg, the immortal island of the dead, which according to Irish mythology—and to Dún Chaoin folklore—was meant to occasionally appear to mortals on the Atlantic horizon. As the poet moves west in the poem, he is following the historical decline of vernacular Irish not just to Dún Chaoin but all the way to its ultimate conclusion, to the extinction of native speech; he journeys so far west in search of the language, in fact, that he arrives at the realm of the dead. In leaving English for Irish, Ó Ríordáin's avatar in the poem is like an epic hero, leaving the land of the living to seek out the voice of his father in the underworld. Like Gabriel Conroy's imagined trip to Connacht in "The Dead," Ó Ríordáin's journey westward in "Return Again," ostensibly to Dún Chaoin, is finally a trip to the deeper, farther west, to "that region where dwell the vast hosts of the dead."[65] Native Irish is now not only next door but, as in Joyce's "The Dead," in the next world.

For all their evocations of the wholesome, timeless natural world which their utopian language communities seem to be unconsciously, organically part of, Ó Ríordáin's Dún Chaoin and Pasolini's Casarsa have something in common with Yeats's Byzantium in "Sailing to Byzantium": a perfect, ageless, poetic place devoid of flesh and blood (an ideal rewritten in the later poem "Byzantium," which brings to the surface the blood and veins pumping beneath the gold enameling).

Heaney was chilled by what he saw as the desire to "obliterate history" in the line "Close your mind to all that has happened since the battle of Kinsale," "Dún d'intinn ar a tharla ó buaileadh Cath Chionn tSáile."[66] Similar charges have been leveled against Pasolini's Friulian poetry.[67] Both Ó Ríordáin and Pasolini seem to be trying to escape history in their minor-language writing—the choice of minor-language mediums seems to be a retreat from the modern world and the realities of history. In each case, specific local historical reasons seem to be behind this desire: Pasolini is seeking refuge from Fascism and embourgoisement, and Ó Ríordáin longs to construct a counterfactual Ireland in which the language and native culture were never supplanted by English. But if the Dún Chaoin of "Return Again" represents the drive to seek out nativeness and perfection, the result of achieving it, of finally "going native," would be to arrive at death. The West is the province of true Irish but also the province of the dead. The death of vernacular Irish is a source of poetic vision, but life is to be found in the linguistic wasteland east of Gleann na nGealt.

Ó Ríordáin identified real Irish and his own poetic program with Dún Chaoin.[68] Yet the true impulse behind this vision was not the language that lived in Dún Chaoin but rather the ghost of the language that had died in English-speaking Ireland—the wasteland that activated his modernist sensibility. As memory of Irish as a living, breathing, daily thing faded in the first decades of the independent Irish state, and as the purity and universality of local dialects in Italy could no longer be taken for granted, these idioms offered themselves as disembodied ghosts of a perfect language, hovering on the edge of day-to-day existence, just out of sight.

The minor literary tradition of lyric poetry in the waning peasant languages of Europe, far removed from the cosmopolitan experiments of Paris, London, and Vienna, and at first glance a last remnant of a premodern world that was bound to fade, was another, later strain of European modernism that deserves a place in our accounts of twentieth-century European culture. Irish in English-speaking Ireland and minor local dialects in the modern industrialized world represented for certain writers the promise of an ideal world next door, *ag béal an dorais,* to this one, a world that could be glimpsed but never reached or inhabited, where the transactions of the marketplace would be conducted in the language of the spirit, where the life of the body would not compromise the purity of the soul, and where the living would share a language with the dead.

four

THE GREAT SILENCE IN COMBRAY:
PROUST AND PATOIS

Proust seems on the face of it an unlikely figure to include in a consideration of how the decline of local dialects and minor languages engaged the modernist literary imagination. He was the product of a thoroughly metropolitan world, born and reared in an imperial capital, a son of a wealthy bourgeois family, and a frequenter of the highest echelons of French and international society. Proust's work is in many ways exemplary of that strain of twentieth-century writing produced by the European upper-middle classes, the kind of world familiar to us from Freud, of small wealthy, professional urban families with servants, townhouses, and country retreats, possessed of an easy cosmopolitan culture. The Gaelic cultural nationalism that was flourishing on the western edge of Europe at the moment when Proust was growing up could not have been more alien from his world. The Gaelic revival valorized all that was untaught, spontaneous, and local, not the product of individual genius but instead springing from an imagined cultural collective. These forms of culture, knowledge, and experience were deeply familiar to Joyce, who grew up in a city that was excitedly engaging with revivalist ideologies, but they were entirely foreign to Proust's intellectual formation. In the society Proust was formed by, the culture to which one aspired was of a transnational, European, "high" kind, produced through thought, reading, and study. In his autobiography, *Die gerettete Zunge* (*The Tongue Set Free*), the Jewish writer Elias Canetti describes a childhood in which his family moves from a city in Bulgaria, to Manchester, to Vienna, and then to Zurich. With each move, the home language of the family changes—Ladino, English, German—and so do elements of local color in the background, always connected with lower social classes—an Armenian woodcutter, Gypsy tradeswomen, local maids. But the family's culture remains the same: Shakespeare, Goethe, Racine.

In the upper-middle-class European milieu of Proust and Canetti, culture is not innately linked to place, to the masses, or to "spontaneous" folk speech but is a product of careful individual refinement.[1] Joyce was never tempted to adopt Irish as a medium for his writing, but he could not avoid the idea, swirling round the intellectual circles of his youth in Dublin, that one might, or could, or should do so; it was not a conclusion one had to agree with but it was not an idea that could be ignored. Idealizations of peasant culture and speech were not part of Proust's cultural world. For Proust's class, local dialects were a folkloric decoration to a fundamentally alien *paysage*, rather than the basis of a pressing political ideology with which one had to engage. The idea that his soul might have best expressed itself in a dialect of farmers and fishermen would have been as wholly, laughably alien to him as it would have been to Virginia Woolf.

Yet, unlike Woolf, Proust was directly confronted with indigenous minor languages and their decline. The old dialects of the French countryside, so-called patois, play a key role in *À la Recherche du temps perdu*, and Proust's unique modernism was subtly but extensively shaped and energized by his exposure to them.[2] Dialect appears in the novel most notably through the housekeeper Françoise—the character with whom the narrator has the longest sustained intimacy—whose mother tongue is the local dialect of Méséglise. The *Atlas linguistique de la France*, compiled in 1897–1900, suggests that, unlike other parts of France where the peasantry was still usually dialect-speaking, the various patois spoken in the area where Proust situated the fictional Combray and Méséglise were becoming extinct at around the time the novel is set, and the disappearance of Françoise's dialect is a minor but persistent theme in the novel.[3]

Patois is one of the many secret languages of the *Recherche*, and like all of them it offers a particular symbolic key for interpreting the world. Along with her unlettered but apparently more authentic way of speaking French, Françoise's dialect comes to seem imbued with the miraculous properties of timelessness for which the novel longs. Her patois has two vital functions in the novel: as one of the few portals to essential, intact realities untouched by the ravages of time, and as a powerful internal challenge to the novel's own high-bourgeois worldview, that is as an energizing alternative to middle-class, novelistic ways of understanding reality.

Joyce's "The Dead" ends with the evocation of a possible "journey westward," but in the story we also see the opposite journey take place, as the Gaelic west comes to Dublin and to Gabriel through the ideological convictions of Molly Ivors. As the ghost of the Gaelic rural west is brought by Miss Ivors to Gabriel, and to the urban, middle-class, English-speaking party in eastern Ireland, in the *Recherche*, Françoise's speech brings the ancient world of the French peasantry to the narrator's city apartments. Unlike Joyce, Proust did not have to confront a political-cultural movement that idealized the dwindling folk cultures of the countryside, and so in the *Recherche* there is no intermediary figure like Miss Ivors to mediate the encounter. Françoise's words, the narrator tells us, bring about "a sort of reverse form of travel whereby it is the countryside that comes to visit the traveler" (III.77, translation modified) ["une sorte de voyage inverse où c'est la villégiature qui vient vers le voyageur" (III.i.57)]. Françoise's way of speaking fills their Parisian apartment in the late nineteenth century with "the country air, the social life of a farm of fifty years ago" (III.77) ["l'air de la campagne et la vie sociale dans une ferme, il y a cinquante ans" (III.i.57)]. And, as in Joyce's story, this linguistic miracle brings the dead in contact with the living: Françoise's words, the narrator tells us, allowed her to "trace her way back as though by clues of coloured thread to the birds and cherry trees of her childhood, to the bed in which her mother had died, and which she still saw" (III.77) ["y retracer comme avec des fils de couleur les cerisiers et les oiseaux de son enfance, le lit où était morte sa mère, et qu'elle voyait encore" (III.i.57–58)].

At different points throughout the novel, the narrator sees a model for his own struggle to find a structure to hold his novel together in Françoise's domestic skills and labor, sometimes sewing or mending, often cooking, for example: "[Perhaps] I should be making my book in the same way that Françoise made that *bœuf à la mode*" [VI.511]) ["ne ferais-je pas mon livre de la façon que Françoise faisait ce bœuf mode" (VIII.340)]. The values of the rural margins that she brings to him enable him to give a form to his content. But she also, less overtly, provides him with a linguistic model, most forcefully of all through her mother tongue, the dialect of Méséglise. Some mysterious property in her language seems to short-circuit the operations of time:

> One could see that the ideas which the mediaeval artist and the medi-aeval peasant (still surviving in the nineteenth century) had of classical and of early Christian history . . . were derived not from books, but from a tradition at once ancient and direct, unbroken, oral, distorted, unrecognisable, and alive. (I.212, translation modified)
> [On sentait que les notions que l'artiste médiéval et la paysanne mé-diévale (survivant au XIXe siècle) avaient de l'histoire ancienne ou chrétienne . . . ils les tenaient non des livres, mais d'une tradition à la fois antique et directe, ininterrompue, orale, déformée, méconnaissa-ble et vivante. (I.149)]

Françoise's native dialect will finally appear to the narrator to possess miraculous qualities that protect it from time altogether. But the narrator's idea that Françoise possesses a precious linguistic heritage alien to his own comes first through his observation of her way of speaking his own language, French. Françoise's command of French is a frequent cause of comment for him, an object, almost simultaneously, of snobbish derision and aesthetic rapture. He often mocks Françoise's mistakes, both with the reader and to her face: "She claimed only one civic right, that of not pronouncing words as we did and of maintaining that 'hôtel,' 'été' and 'air' were of the feminine gender" (V.774–775) ["elle ne réclamait qu'un droit du citoyen, celui de ne pas prononcer comme nous et de maintenir qu'hôtel, été et air étaient du genre féminin" (VI.155)]. While he jeers at her solecisms, at other moments he notices that in her unschooled French, Fran-çoise employs, unbeknownst to herself, the language of the greatest French writers:

> "What is it now they call him?" She broke off as though putting to herself a question of protocol, which she went on to answer with: "Oh,

of course, it's Antoine they call him!" as though Antoine had been a title. "He's the one could tell me, but he's quite the gentleman, he is, a great pedant, you'd think they'd cut his tongue out, or that he'd forgotten to learn to speak. He makes no reply when you talk to him," went on Françoise, who said "make a reply" like Mme de Sévigné. (III.21)

[«Comment donc qu'on lui dit?» s'interrompit-elle comme se posant une question de protocole; elle se répondit à elle-même: «Ah oui! c'est Antoine qu'on lui dit», comme si Antoine avait été un titre. «C'est lui qu'aurait pu m'en dire, mais c'est un vrai seigneur, un grand pédant, on dirait qu'on lui a coupé la langue ou qu'il a oublié d'apprendre à parler. Il ne vous fait même pas réponse quand on lui cause», ajoutait Françoise qui disait: «faire réponse», comme Mme de Sévigné. (III.i.17)]

In her anecdote, Françoise is implicitly contrasting her own ease of speaking with the butler's silence. She hears only the difference between speech and silence, whereas the narrator listening to her story hears peculiarities of language echoing through her words. "Make a reply" comes naturally to Françoise's lips as pure speech; part of the point of the story is that she is unaware of using formulations that were employed by Mme de Sévigné or anyone else. She must be ignorant of the origins or literary connotations of her usage for it to be authentic. As a "nonnative" to Françoise's idiom, the narrator, on the other hand, is able to see what flows through her speech, just as Pasolini felt he perceived marvelous qualities embedded in Livio Socolari's pronunciation of *rosada*, or as Ó Ríordáin's speaker in "Fill Arís" ("Return Again") "sees" grammatical forms shoaling in the sunset. Shortly after this incident, when Françoise is praising the generosity of her old employer, Mme Octave (known to the narrator as Aunt Léonie), the narrator notices that her vocabulary is in part that of the seventeenth century: "Françoise used the word 'spare' in the same sense as La Bruyère" (III.25) ["Françoise employait le verbe 'plaindre' dans le même sens que fait La Bruyère" (III.i.20)].

Françoise's unconscious oral reproduction of the high literary French of several centuries before is in particular contrast with pastiche, the deliberate imitation of style and vocabulary, of which Proust and his narrator are masters, and which runs throughout the *Recherche* (as through *Ulysses*) as a key mode—intellectual, learned, self-consciously allusive—of engaging with the past. Proust began his career as a writer of pastiche, and not only his narrator but several other characters indulge in it throughout the novel. As a modernist technique, pastiche comes from a self-conscious cultural tradition and milieu; Françoise's oblivious use of words, phrases, and grammatical constructions that, to cultivated metropolitan ears, recall the French of great literary masters, offers to the novel an alternative model, instinctive and intuitive, for the transmission of language and culture.

Coming from the metropolitan high bourgeoisie, the narrator has been taught to admire cultivation, including cultivated speech and style. His mother and his grandmother frequently make learned allusions to, precisely, Mme de Sévigné. The genius of Françoise's speech, as the narrator sees it, is attributable not to her, as an individual, or to her own learning or conscious effort, but to something older, bigger, and deeper than any one person; something outside time. The archaeological strata of language and literature that the narrator apprehends in Françoise's speech point to an alternative, oral, "folk" model of culture, in opposition to the acquired, refined, literate culture of Proust's own background, the culture that is so characteristic of the whole of the *Recherche*.

The raptures produced in the narrator by Françoise's French are a countercurrent that challenges the very values on which the novel is based: development, learning, constructing. Her speech appears to embody something the novel longs for: sudden, direct, spontaneous, natural connections outside time and immune to it. This is why the narrator is so troubled when he hears Françoise proudly using items of pretentious trendy slang she picks up from her socially ambitious daughter:

> And as the spirit of imitation, the desire not to appear behind the times, alters the most natural and most positive form of oneself, Fran-

çoise, borrowing the expression from her daughter's vocabulary, used to remark that I was "dippy." She did not like this; she said that I was always "balancing," for when she was not aspiring to rival the moderns, she employed the very language of Saint-Simon. (III.83–84, translation modified)

[Et comme le démon du pastiche, et de ne pas paraître vieux jeu, altère la forme la plus naturelle et la plus sûre de soi, Françoise, empruntant cette expression au vocabulaire de sa fille, disait que j'étais dingo. Elle n'aimait pas cela, elle disait que je « balançais » toujours, car elle usait, quand elle ne voulait pas rivaliser avec les modernes, du langage de Saint-Simon. (III.i.62)]

Here we see two kinds of language at work within Françoise herself, two kinds of language that correspond to two models of culture, and, especially, to two models of cultural continuity. On the one hand, pretentious as it is, using the word *dingo* (a modish slang word for "crazy," which Scott Moncrieff translates as "dippy"), Françoise is being bourgeois, deliberately trying to refine and improve her language by acquiring new words and expressions gleaned from her daughter (who regards herself, the narrator tells us, "as an up-to-date woman who had got out of the old ruts" [IV.172] ["une femme d'aujourd'hui et sortie des sentiers trop anciens" (IV.125)]). This is the vernacular of the daytime, language altered by time and work. On the other hand, in using the synonym that springs to her mind, that he "balances," she is speaking, without realizing it, the language of Saint-Simon, and thus, in the narrator's view, a language of the night, one that, unbeknownst to her, flows through her from the underground springs of history and culture, a language with an immediate connection to centuries past, untouched by and outside time. The full richness inherent in Françoise's linguistic inheritance only comes forth when she is speaking unconsciously, in the dark.

When she employs usages characteristic of Mme de Sévigné or La Bruyère, Françoise is, for the narrator, a cultural vessel for a heritage far older, wider, and deeper than the conscious mind of any individual. What is involved here is not just a different language but a different idea of language, of what constitutes literary or cultural value and how it comes about. Through Françoise's idiom, the narrator imagines he is confronted with an ideal of language not as something wrought or cultivated or worked—as the narrator's style in the *Recherche* so clearly is—but as a living, independent thing that flows, of its own accord, through human channels. In these unconscious linguistic legacies—which, if she had her own conscious way, she would efface entirely in favor of her daughter's chic slang—Françoise puts forward a cultural model that runs counter to the main currents of the *Recherche* and to the ideals of bourgeois metropolitan Europe. Her mode of speech seems to offer an ideal of language, culture, and style that are not products of *Bildung*, of individual talent or training, but that are natural, communal, autonomous phenomena. When she speaks, unawares, the language of Saint-Simon, Françoise points to the nonidentity of individual and language, to the mysterious communal origins and properties of language. These "epiphanies" provoked by Françoise's way of speaking French are part of the central desire of Proust's novel, to isolate and freeze archetypal components of reality outside the flow of time.

The elevation of peasant values is a tricky business in the *Recherche*. The narrator often compares Françoise's habits to those of royalty or celebrated intellectuals and artists: he likens her to Michelangelo when she cooks for M. de Norpois; he tells us that she held the Guermantes family in esteem on the basis of both the number of its branches and the brilliance of its connexions, "as Pascal founds the truth of Religion on Reason and on the authority of the Scriptures" (II.17) ["fondant la grandeur de cette famille à la fois sur le nombre de ses membres et l'éclat de son illustration, comme Pascal, la vérité de la religion sur la raison et l'autorité des Écritures" (III.i.17)].

These juxtapositions of high and low are partly, of course, intended for comic effect—there is more than a hint of mockery in them—as well as to show the universality of patterns and "laws." But when the narrator is talking about Françoise in particular, these comparisons have another, broader application. The novel is acknowledging the limits and the contingency of its high-bourgeois point of view, and the supposedly universal culture—Michelangelo and Pascal—that accompanies it; it is searching for a way to step outside it for a moment. There is no idyll of a lost rural culture that might be sought out or revived circulating in Proust's literary world, but in the mouth of Françoise this peasant culture nonetheless makes itself felt and shapes the novel. In these comparisons, Proust is not only elevating Françoise to the status of great French philosophers or Italian Renaissance artists but also doing something like the reverse: looking, with foreign eyes, to the alien culture of the European peasantry for new models of thought, for ways of energizing and activating his own inner vision. This contact, or imagined contact, with peasant ways of thinking and, especially, speaking, is crucial in linguistic terms for the *Recherche*, in its search, in the darkness and silence, for an unsullied language of the night, uncontaminated by the vernacular daylight.

French, however, is not Françoise's first language. The ultimate version of this idea of language as a phenomenon of nature, immanently connected to the landscape, comes in the evocation of her native language, a dialect restricted to the area around a single small village. Proust's narrator is not a John Millington Synge of the Eure-et-Loir. He has no curiosity about the nature of her patois, its origins, survival, or history, or its meaning for Françoise herself (or for her daughter). He does not decide to learn Françoise's dialect (he eventually learns it by accident, he claims, and just wishes it had been a useful language, "like Persian"), nor does he wish to imitate her way of speaking French. What does capture his interest on the few occasions throughout the novel when Françoise actually converses in her mother tongue suggests a symbolic role for patois and peasant speech that bears upon the major themes of the *Recherche*, however. We know that Françoise's mother tongue differs from that spoken by her daughter and her mother, who grew up in different villages; this in itself is of significance in terms of the *Recherche*'s always energetic interest in forms of inheritance that are independent of the family, for they suggest that our origins and identity come from the earth rather than from our blood. This idea is further reinforced by the fact that here is someone else in the novel who is a native speaker of Françoise's particular dialect:

Miles away . . . there was a small area of France where the people spoke almost precisely the same dialect as in Méséglise. I made this discovery at the same time as I experienced its tediousness, for I once came upon Françoise deep in conversation with a neighbor's house-maid, who came from this village and spoke its dialect. They could more or less understand one other, I could not understand a word, and they knew this but nevertheless continued (excused, they felt, by the joy of being fellow-countrywomen although born so far apart) to converse in this strange tongue in front of me, like people who do not wish to be understood. These picturesque studies in linguistic geography and below-stairs comradeship were renewed weekly in the kitchen, without my deriving any pleasure from them. (IV.173)

[Et, très loin de là, au contraire, il y avait en France une petite région où on parlait presque tout à fait le même patois qu'à Méséglise. J'en fis la découverte en même temps que j'en éprouvai l'ennui. En effet, je trouvai une fois Françoise en grande conversation avec une femme de chambre de la maison, qui était de ce pays et parlait ce patois. Elles se comprenaient presque, je ne les comprenais pas du tout, elles le savaient et ne cessaient pas pour cela, excusées, croyaient-elles, par la joie d'être payses quoique nées si loin l'une de l'autre, de continuer à parler devant moi cette langue étrangère, comme lorsqu'on ne veut pas être compris. Ces pittoresques études de géographie linguistique et de camaraderie ancillaire se poursuivirent chaque semaine dans la cuisine, sans que j'y prisse aucun plaisir. (IV.126)]

This discovery comes in *Sodome et Gomorrhe*, after the narrator has made his discovery of the existence of the gay and lesbian under-worlds. These "picturesque studies in linguistic geography and be-low-stairs comradeship" seem far removed from the narrator's the-ories and taxonomies of "inversion," but they encapsulate some of the same essential ideas. The narrator's discovery of homosexuality comes by chance: he is watching an orchid to see if he might observe its pollination by a bee when he witnesses instead a successful cruis-ing scene between two gay men. The narrator considers the chance encounter of two compatible inverts to be a "miracle" no less natural and amazing than the botanical process of pollination. This linguistic coincidence, of Françoise encountering someone from another part of France who yet speaks Méséglise patois is a "miraculous conjunction" of the same order. The term "camaraderie ancillaire" ("below-stairs comradeship") is itself redolent of the descriptions of secret fellowship and recognition among inverts upon which the narrator expends much time and thought. The hidden universe of mysterious linguistic affinities revealed in this incident, the mutual recognition of these two fellow countrywomen born apart, recalls the invisible "civilizations" of homosexuals to which this volume of the novel is dedicated.

The narrator and the novel always have a lively interest in secret languages and signs. Homosexuality is one of the "keys" that allow the narrator to reinterpret reality: this is one of the main sources of interest for the narrator in the clandestine, esoteric worlds of Sodom and Gomorrah. It is no coincidence that these reflections on incomprehensible rural dialects come in the same volume as those on homosexuality. The most important link between patois and Sodom is the fact that the language in which Françoise and her fellow countrywoman from a distant part of France converse is closed to outsiders and to the narrator; when they speak, the narrator is left in the dark. Initially, this privacy is the only reason for the narrator's interest in their languages. He affects to find the women's unexpected linguistic intimacy to be nothing more than "tedious," but his descriptions of it come very close to his own later aspirations for the kind of language he needs in order to produce his novel.

The idea of patois as a language that can exclude the outside world, remain apart from it, and offer a mental universe protected from it is still clearer at a later moment in the novel, when he describes the linguistic habits of Françoise and her daughter. They only ever spoke to each other in patois, he writes, when they wanted to speak to each other without his understanding them. The normal language of their communication is French—this is how Françoise learns all the fashionable slang the narrator despises—but when they have something secret to say, instead of shutting themselves up in the kitchen, they speak in patois, as "a protective screen more impenetrable than the most carefully closed door" (V.199) ["au lieu d'aller s'enfermer dans la cuisine elles se faisaient, en plein milieu de ma chambre, une protection plus infranchissable que la porte la mieux fermée, en parlant patois" (V.144)].

Once again, the narrator avows a complete lack of interest in his servants' mother tongue per se. He does not say in this passage that his soul speaks patois, or that in the dialect of Méséglise he would find a language corresponding to his inner poetic tongue, but his depiction of the use Françoise and her daughter find for dialect— "they provided themselves, right in the middle of my room, with a protective screen more impenetrable than the most carefully closed door"—approximates his own understanding of what will be required to produce his masterpiece. Like the author's own real-life workroom, sealed against the sounds and sights of daily life, and like his narrator's conviction that a literary work such as he is contemplating can only be produced away and apart from the social world, in this magical property of patois we see a form of exile within, a domestic version of the white martyrdom embraced for their writing, in different ways, by Joyce, Pasolini, and Ó Ríordáin.

This struggle to build an abroad at home points again to a fundamental complementarity between Joyce and Proust. Just as Françoise and her daughter use their private language to create a sealed-off "space" where they are sitting, instead of moving—into physical exile, as it were—in the kitchen, Proust sought to create at home a version of the exile that Joyce found by literally emigrating. Unlike the point of view of an exile like Joyce, which freezes the people and places of youth in memory at a single moment in time, a life like Proust's, led in or around one place, offers a view of the reversals, returns, and development that occur over the course of time. Where *Ulysses* is a book of being, the *Recherche* is one of becoming; *Ulysses* gives us a snapshot of how things are, the *Recherche* shows how things change and develop. The *Recherche* gives an account of how knowledge is acquired and developed through reading and reflection, about how a sensibility is gradually and individually *cultivated*. Development and change are the fundamental realities of the *Recherche*; the challenge for Proust's novel is to identify stable essences outside all this change, to find something solid within all the flux. From within the society, language, and community that constitute the object of his artistic analysis, it is the singularity rather than the collective accumulation of daily life that is elusive. Written from the insider's perspective of the writer at home, the *Recherche* struggles to get outside, to find an exilic point of view from which to capture synchronic reality. We can understand the spasms of involuntary memory that are the key to the novel as one attempted solution to this problem—they freeze reality outside time, just as Joyce's imagination does to Dublin on June 16, 1904, from faraway Trieste, Zurich, and Paris. Swann, the chief mentor of Proust's narrator, is an allegorist, who struggles to fix the faces and personalities he encounters into symbolic figures, always on the hunt for correspondences between people he meets and figures from painting, sculpture, and myths (he sees a resemblance, for example, between the narrator's family's pregnant kitchen maid and Giotto's fresco of Charity). Swann seeks to latch bodies onto eternal forms, as Joyce's imagination does in temporal and spatial exile from his fictional world. Proust's narrator takes after him in this, in his extravagant metaphors and similes, and his taxonomy of "types." For example: "Albertine—and this was perhaps . . . one of the reasons which had made me unconsciously desire her—was one of the incarnations of the little French peasant whose type may be seen in stone at Saint-André-des-Champs" (III.502) ["Albertine—et c'était peut-être . . . une des raisons qui m'avaient à mon insu fait la désirer—était une des incarnations de la petite paysanne française dont le modèle est en pierre à Saint-André-des-Champs" (IV.56)].

At the same time, Swann is also a warning to him about the danger of this kind of allegorization, the blindness and rigidity that it can cause. In the end, the narrator departs from Swann's example, and in the *Recherche* the passage of time and the reality of alteration that is so visible to a writer who, unlike Joyce, spends all his life in his home city among the same people means that no character remains attached to a single mythic correspondence, except in isolated, privileged moments. Neither Albertine nor Odette, for example, is attached to any of the many artistic or allegorical doubles that Swann and the narrator perceive in them. In the end, all of the characters in the *Recherche* ultimately escape the allegorizing attempts of Swann and the narrator (a failure figured by the maddening unfixability—for their boyfriends—of Albertine and Odette).

The experience of certain types of change from which Joyce removed himself by leaving his native country and city, and to which Proust, at home, remained exposed, has an analogous counterpart in the experience of language. In moving to the Continent and speaking Italian even with his own children, Joyce cut himself off from Dublin English as a living, breathing, changing idiom. For Joyce, his English was protected from the processes of normal vernacular change, preserved in the deep freeze of his mind since he left Dublin in 1904. Like its portraits of Bloom and Molly, or its thumbnail sketches of everyone else who passes through his imaginary Dublin on that day, Dublin speech is portrayed in *Ulysses* in once-off detail and accuracy. The life and speech of one day come fully formed into the daylight, from the darkness of Joyce's exiled mind, emerging like a Neolithic body recovered from a peat bog or from the Arctic ice, fully formed and outside time. By contrast, for Proust, French remained the language of both work and life. For Proust, the language he uses in his writing has a lifespan, and it is subject, like the individuals and society depicted in his novel, to the forces of time and change. One of the ways the *Recherche* registers the passage of time is in linguistic vogues and styles that come into and out of fashion; the narrator is fascinated by Odette de Crécy's mania for English words and phrases, and cannot derive pleasure from Mme de Cambremer's refined expressions because "they were those that at are employed in a given period by all the people of the same intellectual range" (IV.438) ["c'étaient celles qu'ont, à une époque donnée, toutes les personnes d'une même envergure intellectuelle" (IV.316)].

The changeability of language is one of the existential panics of Proust's novel, and intuiting the existence of a timeless linguistic core within or underlying the unstable swirl of language in use is one of its great challenges. The mutability of Albertine, a preoccupation across several volumes of the novel, is figured by the ways her language changes over time. The narrator can detect the traces of a change in

her innermost state of mind, or the influence of secret new acquaintances, from "the advent of certain words which had not formed part
of her vocabulary, or at least not in the acceptation which she now
gave them" (III.484) ["l'apparition de certains mots qui ne faisaient
pas partie de son vocabulaire, au moins dans l'acception qu'elle leur
donnait maintenant" (III.ii.44)]. For example, when he hears her
use the word *mousmé*, meaning a girl, a recent import from Japa-
nese, he knows it is proof that she no longer loves him. "Clearly,"
he says, "when I first knew Albertine the word was unknown to her,"
and that "had things followed their normal course, she would never
had learned it" (III.488) ["quand j'avais connu Albertine, le mot de
«mousmé» lui était inconnu . . . si les choses eussent suivi leur cours
normal, elle ne l'eût jamais appris" (III.ii.46–47)]. This "philological
discovery" is proof, the narrator is convinced, that an "internal evolution" has taken place in Albertine, as a consequence of which she is
now indifferent to him.

Albertine's use of the new word, *mousmé*, vexes the narrator in a
way that is superficially different from Françoise's importation of
dingo from her daughter, a vulgar, artificial borrowing alongside the
authentic, natural, fossilized *balancer*. But at heart it is the same question, of linguistic change and conscious—"reflected"—use of new
vocabulary, frustrating the narrator's search for timeless essences and
truths. Albertine's faddish language is only the most outward sign of
her role as the character in the novel who represents the radically
changeable nature of human character, the impossibility of fixing
on any stable sense of a person, or indeed of any reality, that is not
swept away by time. Saint-Loup, similarly, is one of the people in
the novel who turns out to have the least fixed, most fundamentally
alterable nature: the narrator discovers his heterosexuality, his gal-
lantry, his kindness, his refinement all to be overturned at one point
or other in the novel. Saint-Loup's changeability is also registered in
his language:

> Saint-Loup employed in every connexion the verb *faire* for "to have
> the air of," because the spoken language, like the written, feels from

time to time the need of these alterations in the meanings of words, these refinements of expression. And just as journalists often have not the least idea what school of literature the "turns of phrase" they use originate from, so the vocabulary, the very diction of Saint-Loup were formed in imitation of three different aesthetes none of whom he knew but whose modes of speech had been indirectly inculcated into him. (III.87–88)

[Saint-Loup employait à tout propos ce mot de «faire» pour «avoir l'air», parce que la langue parlée, comme la langue écrite, éprouve de temps en temps le besoin de ces altérations du sens des mots, de ces raffinements d'expression. Et de même que souvent les journalistes ignorent de quelle école littéraire proviennent les «élégances» dont ils usent, de même le vocabulaire, la diction même de Saint-Loup étaient faits de l'imitation de trois esthètes différents dont il ne connaissait aucun, mais dont ces modes de langage lui avaient été indirectement inculqués. (III.i.65)]

The degenerative action of time upon language is experienced most painfully by the narrator in the language of Françoise, the only character to whom he is close throughout the novel, indeed one of the few to last at all from the beginning to the end. Françoise's speech in its ideal form offers the narrator a contrasting model of stability and continuity, an ideal of an immutable and ageless form of language. As the narrator remembers it, her original way of speaking French, unconscious and instinctive, seems to be outside time, a medium in which the language of Mme de Sévigné and La Bruyère, as well as the spirit of medieval France, is transmitted. In its timeless purity, it is the implicit opposite of the changeful language of Albertine. But toward the end of her life, the narrator bitterly laments the corrosive effects the years have had on Françoise's speech:

For in her humility, in her affectionate admiration for people infinitely inferior to herself, she had come to adopt their ugly habits of speech. Her daughter having complained to me about her and having used the words (I do not know where she had heard them): "She's always finding fault with me because I don't close the doors properly and *patatipatali* and *patatapatala*," Françoise doubtless thought only her insufficient education that had deprived her until now of this beautiful idiom. And from those lips which I had once seen bloom with the purest French I heard several times a day, "*Et patatipatali patatapatala.*" (VI.86)

[Car dans son humilité, dans sa tendre admiration pour des êtres qui lui étaient infiniment inférieurs, elle adoptait leur vilain tour de langage. Sa fille s'étant plainte d'elle à moi et m'ayant dit (je ne sais de qui elle l'avait reçu): « Elle a toujours quelque chose à dire, que je ferme mal les portes, et patatipatali et patatapatala », Françoise crut sans doute que son incomplète éducation seule l'avait jusqu'ici privée de ce bel usage. Et sur ses lèvres où j'avais vu fleurir jadis le français le plus pur j'entendis plusieurs fois par jour: « Et patatipatali et patatapatala». (VII.56–57)]

The phrase "those lips which I had once seen bloom with the purest French" is redolent of Ó Ríordáin's grammatical vision at the end of "Fill Arís" ("Return Again"), and the suggestion that this French was corrupted out of a misplaced desire for respectability has echoes with Fr. Tomás Ó Ceallaigh's description of language change in late nineteenth-century Sligo: "When these people married they taught their children not the old speech that was as honey on their lips, but the English which with so much pain they had acquired. They had been brought up in the belief that English was the top-notch of respectability, the key that opened Sesame."[4] In the *Recherche*, social ambition and social advancement are the very epitome of mutability, and especially of the fact that categories and situations which appear to be fixed and unalterable are not. In an essay on the language spoken by servants in the *Recherche*, Chip Long notes that "Françoise's speech before her corruption evokes the premodern world of aristocratic hegemony in which social mobility was virtually nonexistent."[5] Once Françoise is aware of the words she is using and deliberately seeks, like Odette, Albertine, Mme de Cambremer, or Saint-Loup, to improve or beautify it, once she is no longer speaking in the dark, the tongue of the past and the rhythm of the French classics no longer, as the narrator sees it, speak through her:

> Her daughter's influence was beginning to contaminate Françoise's vocabulary. . . . For this decadence of Françoise's speech, which I had known in its golden period, I was in fact myself indirectly responsible.

Françoise's daughter would not have made her mother's classic language degenerate into the vilest slang if she had stuck to conversing with her in dialect. (V.199)
[L'influence de sa fille commençait à altérer un peu le vocabulaire de Françoise. . . . Cette décadence du parler de Françoise, que j'avais connu à ses belles époques, j'en étais, du reste, indirectement responsable. La fille de Françoise n'aurait pas fait dégénérer jusqu'au plus bas jargon le langage classique de sa mère, si elle s'était contentée de parler patois avec elle. (V.144)]

It is this fact—that if Françoise and her daughter had conversed in patois, Françoise's pure French would have been preserved—that caused the narrator to discuss patois in the first place. He has no apparent interest in the actual content of their dialect, other than the vague knowledge that the forms of it they spoke differed slightly from one another. The only words that are ever directly quoted in it are *m'esasperate*, which he is not fully able to decipher, and *poutana*, muttered by Françoise in relation to Albertine. But dialect has a powerful symbolic role as an idealized form of language that is wholly cut off and preserved from the corrosions and corruptions of time, and its twin, society.

Proust's insistence on the radical distinction between voluntary and involuntary memory is structurally equivalent to Croce's "reflected" versus "spontaneous" use. The distinction between involuntary speech, like Françoise's patois or her "pure," instinctive French, and deliberately cultivated language is of the same order as that between involuntary and voluntary memory. The miracle of patois, like that of the taste of the madeleine or the feel of an uneven paving stone underfoot, which transports the narrator to a wholly intact moment of the past, is that it is change-proof, pure, uncontaminated and uncontaminatable by time. Of course, like Irish for Ó Ríordáin and Friulian for Pasolini, this is an artistic ideal, not a philological reality; had the narrator really spoken Françoise's patois, or heard her speak it when she was younger, or had he heard her elderly neighbors back home in Méséglise speaking it, he would doubtless have found it degraded and polluted by interference from standard French.

Patois has a symbolic role in the novel as a model of internal exile, a bubble protected from the vulgarizing vernacular transformations of metropolitan French and its vain social world, and even from the operations of time altogether. But it is also illuminating in terms of the theme of social desire and ambition, a theme that provides the novel with much of its plot. Françoise's French is denatured by a bourgeois form of social ambition, alien to her deeper peasant nature, whereas her native patois, in the narrator's eyes wholly protected from that kind of aspiration, remains pure and unpolluted. Class, and projections provoked by class, are an essential component of this imaginative construction: peasant culture in its true, uncompromised form, seems to the narrator unsusceptible to this kind of change. Part of this, as for Pasolini or Ó Ríordáin, comes from a sense of rural life and peasant culture as being the antithesis of *progress* of all kinds, whether industrialization, linguistic evolution, social success, or material advancement.

Investment, cultivation, growth, aspiration, and change are the features of middle-class life and operations of time. In opposition to the changeful French of the socially mobile middle classes stands not only the vernacular of the peasantry but also of that of the aristocracy. Although it was not as true in France as it was in Italy that peasants and nobility spoke dialect while the bourgeoisie or tradesmen were attached to the standard, the French aristocracy did remain very much associated with dialect and local forms of speech. Indeed, Auguste Brun writes that the reason the Revolution was so hostile to patois was because local dialects somehow had a whiff of feudalism about them, a "survival from the feudal past [une survivance du passé, du passé féodal]."[6] Yeats's and Gregory's fantasy of an Irish-speaking Ireland also retained a nostalgic feudal residue, the old language reestablishing the ancient bond between the aristocracy and the peasantry as a bulwark against a materialistic Anglophone Catholic middle class.[7]

The aristocracy and the peasantry share a connection, whether actual or symbolic, to the land and nature, to place-names, topography, agriculture, and cultural continuity. Already the narrator's interest in

Françoise's patois was linked to what Genette calls his "cratylism," the dream of a motivated connection between words and things, in this case between language (or culture) and nature (as opposed to bourgeois artifice and artistry).[8] Françoise's mother tongue, the patois of Méséglise, is a foreign language to the narrator but native to the place where his family is from and where he spends much of his childhood. Françoise's words seem to him to be mystically linked to the natural world, to landscape, terrain, vegetation, the earth, and to the minute specificities of local places. When he is discussing the two distinct dialects spoken by Françoise herself and by her mother, who had grown up in a neighboring village, he attributes the differences to variations in the natural landscape: "[Their] dialects differed slightly, like the two landscapes, Françoise's mother's village, on a slope descending into a ravine, being overgrown with willows" (IV.173) ["les patois différaient légèrement comme les deux paysages. Le pays de la mère de Françoise, en pente et descendant à un ravin, était fréquenté par les saules" (IV.126)]. These characteristics of her language are in obvious contrast with his own universalizing French, which cannot be rooted or located in any given place or considered to be the product of any individual landscape.

These reflections on patois and on a folk model of linguistic inheritance are exceptional moments, when the narrator's eye is turned toward the uncultured rural poor. His gaze is more often fixed on classes above him, and especially on aristocrats, whom he admires from his earliest childhood and his social success with whom provides one of the principal narrative engines of the novel. And indeed some of the same characteristics attributed to the language of the peasantry are extended to the speech of the old aristocracy. In the linguistic micro-universe of the old French nobility, the narrator sees something of a similar vision of unconsciously embodied communal history and culture, an organic connection between the individual, culture, and the natural landscape. In certain aristocrats—only the very purest and most thoroughbred of them—the narrator finds the same epiphanic flashes of history and culture that he perceives in Françoise. The other character whom the narrator describes as speaking an organic, folk form of French, through which the history of France, its literature, and its natural landscape can be perceived together, is the arch-aristocrat and society celebrity, the duchesse de Guermantes, whose speech and voice, the narrator tells us, seem to sprout organically from the land:

> In [the Duchess's] eyes and . . . voice, I recognized much of the life of nature round Combray. Certainly, in the affectation with which that voice betrayed at times a rudeness of the soil, there was more than one element: the wholly provincial origin of one branch of the Guermantes family, which had for long remained more localized, more hardy, wilder, more combative than the rest . . . and the habit of nobles who fraternise more readily with their peasants than with the middle classes. . . . She rarely strayed beyond the pure vocabulary that might have been used by an old French writer. And when one was tired of the composite patchwork of modern speech, it was very restful to listen to Mme de Guermantes's talk, even though one knew it could express far fewer things—almost as restful, if one was alone with her and she restrained and clarified the flow of her speech still further, as listening to an old song. Then, as I looked at and listened to Mme de Guermantes, I could see, imprisoned in the perpetual afternoon of her eyes, a sky of Île-de-France or of Champagne spread itself, grey-blue, oblique. . . . (III.677–679)
>
> [Dans ces yeux . . . et dans cette voix je retrouvais beaucoup de la nature de Combray. Certes, dans l'affectation avec laquelle cette voix faisait apparaître par moments une rudesse de terroir, il y avait bien des choses: l'origine toute provinciale d'un rameau de la famille de Guermantes, resté plus longtemps localisé, plus hardi, plus sauvageon, plus provocant; puis l'habitude de . . . nobles fraternisant plus volontiers avec leurs paysans qu'avec des bourgeois . . . Elle n'usait guère que du pur vocabulaire dont eût pu se servir un vieil auteur français. Et quand on était fatigué du composite et bigarré langage moderne, c'était, tout en sachant qu'elle exprimait bien moins de choses, un grand repos d'écouter la causerie de Mme de Guermantes,—presque le même, si l'on était seul avec elle et qu'elle restreignît et clarifiât encore son flot, que celui qu'on éprouve à entendre une vieille chanson. Alors en regardant, en écoutant Mme de Guermantes, je voyais, prisonnier dans la perpétuelle et quiète après-midi de ses yeux, un ciel d'Île-de-France ou de Champagne se tendre, bleuâtre, oblique. . . . (III.ii.178–179)]

The Duchess's language, the "almost rustic speech of the old no-bility" (III.265) ["le ton presque paysan de l'ancienne aristocratie" (III.i.190)], is of a similar order to patois, immanently bound to a particular place, arising from and embodying a natural landscape and a cultural tradition, as though they were inseparable from one another. As with Françoise, these traces of ancient origins in her speech are only perceptible at certain, privileged moments. At these moments, the narrator perceives in her pronunciations and phrasings something of what Pasolini saw in unwritten Friulian dialects, or Ó Ríordáin in the Irish of Dún Chaoin: an immemorial *meanma* of people, culture, and landscape fused together and wholly immune to time, a form of language that resists the accumulations and distortions of passing time and thus appears to offer a portal of immediate access to historically distant moments, and a example of an immanent connection between culture and nature.

Moreover, just as the stable, eternal core that could be discerned in Françoise's spoken idiom was contrasted with the evolving, rootless, unstable French of her daughter and niece (and that of Albertine), the timeless essence contained within the Duchess's language is opposed to the carefully cultivated, modern speech of her nephew, Saint-Loup:

> From her accent, her choice of words, one felt that the basis of the Duchess's conversation came directly from Guermantes. In this way, the Duchess differed profoundly from her nephew Saint-Loup, impregnated by so many new ideas and expressions. (III.688–689)
> [À l'accent, au choix des mots on sentait que le fond de conversation de la duchesse venait directement de Guermantes. Par là, la duchesse différait profondément de son neveu Saint-Loup, envahi par tant d'idées et d'expressions nouvelles. (III.ii.186)]

This idea of the peasantry and the aristocracy as a double alternative to middle-class progress is caught up with genre, with the fraught question of what kind of book the *Recherche* is and what kind of book it aspires to be. In Françoise's patois and—before it is corrupted—in her French, as well as in the speech of the Duchess, the narrator is confronted with an alternative not only to his own way of speaking French but to bourgeois culture itself and to its principles, to acquired, written culture, to classical learning and to the sacred middle-class European doctrine of *Bildung*, of cultural, linguistic, and spiritual *cultivation*. It is not too much of a stretch to see a parallel here with the unselfawareness and instinctiveness Ó Ríordáin and Pasolini idolize in the native speakers of their respective adopted minor languages. In these epiphanic moments observed in the speech of Françoise or the Duchess, the narrator sees, to use Croce's term, *uso spontaneo*, spontaneous usage, in sharp contrast to his own highly elaborated and self-conscious *uso riflesso* (and what novel could be more *riflesso* and constructed than the *Recherche?*).

In the case of both the uneducated Françoise and the highly literate duchesse de Guermantes, the narrator associates linguistic richness with lack of knowledge, a lack of formal intellectual instruments and learning. The ancient underground waters that flow through Françoise's mind manifest themselves mostly in her errors and ignorance. The narrator tells us that "she knew nothing, in that absolute sense in which to know nothing means to understand nothing, except the rare truths to which the heart is capable of directly attaining. The vast world of ideas did not exist for her" (II.309) ["Elle ne savait rien, dans ce sens total où ne rien savoir équivaut à ne rien comprendre, sauf les rares vérités que le cœur est capable d'atteindre directement. Le monde immense des idées n'existait pas pour elle" (II.208)]. More surprisingly, in the case of the Duchess's language, the narrator observes that

it is difficult, when one's mind is troubled by the ideas of Kant and the yearnings of Baudelaire, to write the exquisite French of Henri IV, so that the very purity of the Duchess's language was a sign of limitation and that, in her, both intelligence and sensibility had remained closed against innovation. (III.689)

[il est difficile, quand on est troublé par les idées de Kant et la nostalgie de Baudelaire, d'écrire le français exquis d'Henri IV, de sorte que la pureté même du langage de la duchesse était un signe de limitation,

et qu'en elle l'intelligence et la sensibilité étaient restées fermées à
toutes les nouveautés. (III.ii.186)]

In the language of Françoise and the duchesse de Guermantes,
the narrator witnesses not only linguistic diversity but also irreduc-
ibly different ways of seeing, knowing, and understanding, a whole
mode of being in the world that is alien to his middle-class universe.
The purity, authenticity, and ancient continuity of their speech is
connected to a lack of education, an absence of formal instruction
or breadth of learning; this lack gives them access to something else
that cannot be acquired through any deliberate cultivation or effort,
something that can only be transmitted natively. This linguistic nativeness is part of the general longing in the novel for a dimension of
experience that is not worked on, not shaped, wrought, or denatured
by reflection or by time. But the atavistic linguistic spirit that the
narrator sees in Françoise and the Duchess also represents a feudal
alternative to the *novel*. The novel is the genre of the middle classes,
the genre of aspiration, cultivation, work, development, and change.
The *Recherche*, so exceptional in other ways, is an emblematic example of this. Novels follow middle-class dreams of social advancement
and middle-class fears of economic distress; they are animated by the
wish for or fear of a substantive change of one's social and economic
place in the world. The Cinderella plot, the romance of marrying
nobility and leaving the bourgeoisie for the aristocracy—the dream
achieved in the *Recherche* by Mme Verdurin—is, practically by definition, a middle-class one.

The vestiges of older, timeless forms of language in the feudal
classes run counter to the fantasy of social ascent that gives the *Recherche* its plot. At the time of the French Revolution, patois was
considered a feudal relic, the antithesis of social mobility. Speaking
dialect was similarly the definition of uncouthness; Brun recalls that
in his own childhood, "for a middle-class woman . . . it would have
been as indecent to speak a sentence in patois as to utter a swear-
word [pour une femme de la bourgeoisie . . . il eût été aussi indécent
de prononcer une phrase en patois que d'émettre un juron]."[9] The

spread of the standard language at the expense of dialect or minor rural languages is, in an obvious concrete sense, a sign of historical change and progress, of industrialization, communications technology, social evolution. But in literary terms it is also the sign of time and change in a more symbolic sense; as the language of *manners*, the language of the bourgeoisie, it is the sign of social aspiration, self-improvement, of change itself—the language of the novel and not the language of lyric poetry. Proust's novel aspires to the condition of lyric poetry in the full knowledge that it can never attain it. This brings us back to the idea that turned out to be so inescapable in Ireland and elsewhere: that "rediscovered" minor languages and dialects were a modernist solution for lyric poetry, the creation of an autonomous world disconnected from history and from secular— vernacular—time, but could not really function in the same way as creative mediums for prose. Thus, in the *Recherche*, patois and ancient rural speech survivals like it remain a necessary but unachievable utopian ideal of a reality outside time, of a novel that longs to "go native" to lyric but is always cast back on its fallen, prosaic world.

Proust's treatment of time thus has a resonance with the political beliefs that partly underwrote Pasolini's use of Friulian—a conviction that the inexorable rise of the bourgeoisie would bring about a moralistic deadening of human culture and expressivity, and a longing for the spontaneous, carnal reality he saw in the world embodied by dialect. What Pasolini saw in dialect was also a vision of timelessness, a purified reality untouched by progress, cultivation, or development, a modern dream of lyric poetry. One of the chief elements that drew Ó Ríordáin and Pasolini to their minor languages as literary mediums was a desire for a language that might be unsullied by history: Ó Ríordáin longs for a counterfactual possible world for Irish that might have existed had Kinsale turned out differently, Pasolini for a language untouched by Fascism, industrialization, and bourgeois homogenization.

In the end, however, even Françoise's French, through which flowed the words of Mme de Sévigné and the spirit of medieval France, turns out, like everything else in the novel that seemed to be eternal, to be susceptible to the ravages of time. It, too, is finally changed, polluted, and debased, transformed into the time-bound, aspirational, bourgeois vernacular, into *patatipatali patatapatala*. And in the end even Françoise, like the rest of France, abandons her native patois. The Friulian-speaking world will gradually be folded into a modernized, bourgeois Italy, English will creep farther west along the Corca Dhuibhne peninsula from Gleann na nGealt and push Irish into the sea. For Proust, as for Pasolini and Ó Ríordáin, it is the unrealizable promise of an escape from the fallen world that is the key creative property of the dying languages of the countryside.

NOTES

Preface

1. For accounts of the theory and practice of this project, see for example, Eric Hayot, *On Literary Worlds* (New York: Oxford University Press, 2012); Jessica Berman, *Modernist Commitments: Ethics, Politics, and Transnational Modernism* (New York: Columbia University Press, 2011); Emily Apter, *Against World Literature* (New York: Verso, 2013).

2. Michael Cronin points out that this overlooked phenomenon undermines widely held postcolonial views of linguistic history: "The signal failure to account for the linguistic and translational complexity of Europe in part stems from the tendency by post-colonial critics to reduce Europe to two languages, English and French, and to two countries, England and France. Thus, the critique of imperialism becomes itself imperialist in ignoring or marginalizing the historical and translation experience of most European languages. . . . The reductionism and partiality that are implicit in essentialist accounts of the European translation experience are all the more regrettable in that minority languages in Europe offer graphic illustrations of the processes of conquest, resistance and selfdefinition that guide translation in its relationship with power and history." Michael Cronin, "Altered States: Translation and Minority Languages," *TTR: Traduction, terminologie, rédaction*, 8, no. 1, 1995, pp. 85–86.

3. Still less is it a case of what Alexander Beecroft calls the "epichoric," a local literary tradition operating in isolation from other, larger, literatures, where the local language is the only one available to literature. See Beecroft, "World Literature Without a Hyphen: Towards a Typology of Literary Systems, *New Left Review* 54 (Nov.–Dec. 2008), pp. 87–100.

Introduction

1. Seán Ó Ríordáin, "An Ghaeltacht agus fairsingiú na teangan," *Comhar* 13, no. 12 (December 1954), p. 10.

2. See Seán de Fréine, *The Great Silence* (Cork: Mercier Press, 1978), pp. 64–65.

3. See Catherine Matheson and David Matheson, *Educational Issues in the Learning Age* (London: Continuum, 2000), pp. 20–21.

4. De Fréine speculates (*The Great Silence*, p. 65) that the lack of testimony with regard to the language shift is "largely a consequence of the event itself."

5. Pádraig Ó Riagáin, "Irish Language Production and Reproduction 1981–1996," in *Can Threatened Languages Be Saved? Reversing Language Shift, Revisited: A 21st Century Perspective*, ed. Joshua A. Fishman (Clevedon: Multilingual Matters, 2000), p. 197. My own study of the figures shows that for some reason an unusual amount of obviously English-speaking Protestant families, all over the country, returned themselves as Irish-speaking monoglots in 1901 and 1911. To date I have not found an adequate explanation for this.

6. Although Ó Riagáin argues that, despite various margins of error, the census figures can still provide a useful basis for analysis. See Pádraig Ó Riagáin, *Language Policy and Social Reproduction: Ireland 1893–1993* (Oxford: Clarendon Press; New York: Oxford University Press, 1997), pp. 4–7.

7. The first assumption might be that the 1911 entry is a sign of a desire for upward mobility (I cannot help but see the more definite entries for "English only" in the more literate home of my great-grandfather's future wife, my great-grandmother, as a sign of slightly higher social standing or ambition). But in the 1901 census, two young relatives who are staying in the house are recorded, in distinction to my great-grandfather and his siblings, as knowing English only, suggesting that the linguistic descriptions are deliberate and considered. The uncertainty may mean that he had spoken some Irish in childhood, perhaps only with his father, before the family switched over completely to English, and that the little he knew he had forgotten by 1911. But this raises more questions than it answers: how would one forget Irish living in a community where it remained in use among large sections of the population, when one had spoken it at the age of seventeen, and when one was still living alone with a parent for whom it was a native language? In her analysis of language shift on the island of Cape Clear in Co. Cork, Máire Ní Chiosáin identifies a number of reliably reported bilinguals in 1901 returned as monoglots, of either language, in 1911. Those who switched from Irish and English to Irish alone had an average age

of nearly sixty in the earlier return—presumably elderly people whose English became rusty as they had less and less need to call on it in for trade, travel, or bureaucracy. The number who shifted from English and Irish to English alone constitute only a small number of individuals, with a mean age of ten and a half—seven years younger than my great-grandfather—in 1911. See Máire Ní Chiosáin, "Language Shift in Early Twentieth-Century Ireland," *Proceedings of the Harvard Celtic Colloquium* 26/27 (2006/2007), pp. 374–375.

8. The 1911 figures in particular need to be viewed with caution, however. Many seem more inclined to list either English or Irish when there was bilingualism—e.g., several families are listed with monoglot Irish-speaking parents and monoglot English-speaking children, an obvious impossibility. Perhaps it is that once the language shift was consolidated, when filling in the census people were branded as belonging to one linguistic generation or another, the Irish speakers or the English speakers.

9. Ní Chiosáin ("Language Shift," p. 374) notes that if the census returns are accurate, there were several households on Cape Clear where children and old people could not understand each other.

10. Quoted by de Fréine, *The Great Silence*, p. 74.

11. The violence with which revivalist interest in Irish was confronted and the shame, anger, and bitterness with which the language was regarded by the native speakers themselves are evident in anecdotes from Wagner's research. In the early 1950s, for example, Wagner was persuaded to go to Glenlark in Co. Tyrone (where my own ancestors were among the last native speakers of Sperrin Irish). Through a chimney, he heard Irish being spoken in a family cabin, but when he approached, and before he even announced his mission, a ragged woman leaped out, screaming at him: "Away you go. . . . There's no Irish here. Be off. We're all Irish here but we have no Irish an' want no Irish." The woman's sister later whispered to Wagner that they were Irish speakers, but that her sister, the ragged woman, had been an emigrant in Brooklyn and was still traumatized by the humiliations visited upon her by other Irish immigrants for speaking Irish. Michael J. Murphy, *Tyrone Folk Quest* (Belfast: Blackstaff Press, 1973), pp. 66–67.

12. In keeping with the practice of Irish teaching in Ireland, students from Ulster, Connacht, or Munster learned a standardized version of the dialect of their home province. But they did not connect this with their own localities; my grandmother used to refer (disparagingly) to the fact that

my grandfather, from Co. Clare, spoke "Kerry" Irish. By this she meant Munster Irish, of which Clare Irish, when it was alive, was a subvariety. She thought of it as Kerry Irish because Kerry was where the Munster-Irish speaking Gaeltacht was located; this apparently casual question of nomenclature, however, shows just how much the source of Irish had been shifted onto the Gaeltacht and out of the places from which the language had only very recently disappeared (and in the case of Clare, where native speakers were still to be found in reasonable numbers, the last known native speaker from Doolin dying in 1987).

13. In the Gaeltacht of this time, the 1930s, English was still, however, the language of opportunity. And Irish may to some extent have been a language of advancement for English speakers rather more in the lower-middle classes and in the lower grades of the civil service, where my grandparents worked, than higher up.

14. See Eugen Weber, *Peasants into Frenchmen: The Modernization of Rural France, 1870–1914* (Palo Alto: Stanford University Press, 1976), pp. 67–68.

15. W. Theodor Elwert, "Letterature nazionali e letterature dialettali nell'Europa occidentale," *Paideia* 25 (1970), p. 172.

16. Rebecca Posner, *The Romance Languages* (Cambridge: Cambridge University Press, 1996), p. 333.

17. Martin Lyons, "Politics and Patois: The Linguistic Policy of the French Revolution," *Australian Journal of French Studies* XVIII, no. 3 (1981), p. 264.

18. As Eric Hobsbawm points out, national languages are, almost by definition, "semi-artificial constructs." *Nations and Nationalism Since 1780* (Cambridge: Cambridge University Press, 1990), p. 54.

19. François Héran, Alexandra Filhon, and Christine Deprez, "Language Transmission in France in the Course of the 20th Century," *Population & Sociétés* no. 376 (2002), p. 4.

20. For example, all of the many peasant characters in Stendhal's *Le Rouge et le noir* (1830) must be speakers of Francoprovençal. Diglossia and code-switching must have been a characteristic of everyday life in the Jura at the time, but dialect receives only the briefest of mentions in the novel.

21. Elwert, "Letterature nazionali e letterature dialettali nell'Europa occidentale," p. 184.

22. Tradition names Dolly Pentreath of Mousehole, near Penzance, who died in 1777, as the last native speaker of Cornish, but—as with some of Wagner's informants on extinct dialects of Irish in the 1940s and

1950s—there remained individuals, perhaps well into the nineteenth century, who had acquired some knowledge of the language through their grandparents, at sea with older fishermen, or otherwise indirectly. For an account of these, and of the history, decline, and attempted revival of Cornish, see Philip Payton, "Cornish," in *Languages in Britain and Ireland*, ed. Glanville Price (Oxford: Blackwell, 2000), pp. 109–118.

23. See Janet Davies, "Welsh," in *Languages of Britain and Ireland*, ed. Price, pp. 89–96.

24. See Kenneth MacKinnon, "Scottish Gaelic," in *Languages of Britain and Ireland*, ed. Price, pp. 45–49.

25. Werner F. Leopold, "Low German: A Receding Language," *German Quarterly* 34, no. 2 (March 1961), pp. 123–133, and "The Decline of German Dialects," *Word* XV (1959), pp. 130–153.

26. "La tradizione dialettale registra oggi un'imprevedibile rinnovamento poetico, che cade in coincidenza con la crisi più grave mai vissuta dai dialetti a livello dell'uso." Franco Brevini, "Introduzione," *Poeti dialettali del Novecento*, p. vi, quoted in John P. Welle, "Pasolini's Friulian Academy, Dialect Poetry, and Translation Studies," *Romance Languages Annual 1990* 2, pp. 286–290.

27. Peredur Lynch, "Twentieth Century Welsh Literature," in *Celtic Literatures in the Twentieth Century*, ed. Séamus Mac Mathúna, Ailbhe Ó Corráin, and Maxim Fomin (Belfast: Research Institute for Irish and Celtic Studies, 2007), p. 97

28. Francis Favereau, "Twentieth Century Breton Literature," in *Celtic Literatures in the Twentieth Century*, ed. Mac Mathúna, Ó Corráin, and Fomin, p. 130.

29. For an account of how folklore is predicated on the death of tradition, and how narratives of decline and endangerment are central to Irish nation building, see Diarmuid Ó Giolláin, *Locating Irish Folklore* (Cork: Cork University Press, 2000).

30. Gilles Deleuze and Félix Guattari, "Minor Literature: Kafka," in *The Deleuze Reader*, ed. Constantin Boundas (New York: Columbia University Press, 1993), p. 152.

31. Ó Ríordáin in fact criticized Irish poetry in English—a classic case of minor literature in Deleuze and Guattari's terms—for being excessively territorialized: "The fault I see with the English-language literary tradition in Ireland is that it is too centered on Ireland, always talking about Ireland, and about my father and about the field back home when I was young, and that kind of thing [Is é an locht a chímse ar thraidisiún

scríbhneoireachta an Bhéarla in Éirinn go bhfuil sé ró-Éireannach, ag tagairt d'Éirinn i gcónaí, agus do m'athair agus don ghort ag baile nuair a bhíos óg agus rudaí mar sin]." Ó Ríordáin, "Tagann na rudaí ar ais chugat" ["Things come back to you"], *Comhar* 46, no. 2 (February 1987), p. 30.

32. Quoted by Tomás Ó Fiaich in *The Course of Irish History*, ed. T. W. Moody and F. X. Martin (Cork: Mercier Press, 1967), p. 62.

33. And in any case, native speakers of rural vernaculars are often more at ease reading in the major language than in their own. Albert Dauzat noted this with regard to French dialects: "How often I have seen peasants who can read French with ease struggle to decipher an article, usually of humorous nature, printed in patois in the local newspaper! [Que de fois ai-je vu des paysans qui lisaient couramment le français ahaner pour déchiffrer un article, généralement humoristique, imprimé en patois dans le journal local!]" Dauzat, *Les Patois* (Paris: Delagrave, 1927), p. 59.

34. Heinrich Wagner, *Linguistic Atlas and Survey of Irish Dialects*, 4 vols. (Dublin: Dublin Institute for Advanced Studies, 1958–1964), vol. I, p. x.

Chapter 1. Language of the Dead

1. Page references for quotations from Joyce are to the following editions: *Dubliners* [1914] (New York: Penguin, 2000), *A Portrait of the Artist as a Young Man* [1916] (New York: Penguin, 2000), *Ulysses* [1922], ed. Hans Walter Gabler (London: Vintage, 1986), and *Finnegans Wake* [1939] (New York: Penguin, 2000). References to *Ulysses* are given as chapter and line number.

2. W. J. McCormack draws a connection between the mysterious words uttered on the deathbed in "Eveline" and Molly Ivors's challenge to Gabriel about the Irish language in "The Dead," as "moments when the dead language asserts itself in Joyce's English." See W. J. McCormack, "James Joyce, Cliché, and the Irish Language," in *James Joyce: The Augmented Ninth*, ed. Bernard Benstock (Syracuse: Syracuse University Press, 1988), pp. 323–336.

3. One informant, for example, maintains that the phrase might be a phonetic rendering of *do raibh ann, siar ann*, which she translates as "(some) one has gone there, (one must) go (back) there." The Joyce scholar Wim Tigges writes: "Not only does this explanation, in spite of its slight ambiguity, seem to be less 'corrupt' than the ones quoted by Gif-

ford, but in view of the major theme of 'Eveline,' the dilemma of staying or going, it also appears to me eminently appropriate." Wim Tigges, "'Derevaun Seraun!': Resignation or Escape?" *James Joyce Quarterly* 32, no. 1 (1994), pp. 103–104. Alas, Tigges's enthusiasm is misplaced. *Do raibh ann, siar ann* not only means nothing of the sort, it actually means nothing at all, being a mixture of unconnected verb forms and deictics with no possible syntactical linkage. The commonly cited hypothesis that it means "the end of pleasure is pain" is equally outlandish (cited in William Y. Tindall, *A Reader's Guide to James Joyce* [New York: Noonday Press, 1959], p. 22).

4. Different prepositions are used to take leave in Irish, depending on whether the speaker is the person leaving or staying. In this case, since Molly Ivors is the one departing the company and leaving her interlocutors behind, she ought more accurately to say *Beannacht agaibh* rather than *Beannacht libh*. W. J. McCormack makes much of this mistake as a suggestion that "it is really Gabriel who is setting out on his journey westward," which makes some sense but may assume too much knowledge of the Irish language on Joyce's part. McCormack, "James Joyce, Cliché, and the Irish Language," pp. 332–333.

5. For an account of the sociolinguistic situation in the Gaeltacht see Joe Mac Donnacha, "The Death of a Language," *Dublin Review of Books* 50 (February 24, 2014).

6. Parts of the Cooley Peninsula in Co. Louth, just sixty miles north of Dublin, were still Irish-speaking in 1904.

7. Nuala Ní Dhomhnaill, "Why I Choose to Write in Irish, the Corpse That Sits Up and Talks Back," *New York Times Book Review*, January 8, 1995, pp. 3, 27–28.

8. Mary Daly, "Literacy and Language Change in the Late Nineteenth and Early Twentieth Centuries," in *The Origins of Popular Literacy in Ireland: Language Change and Educational Development, 1700–1920*, ed. Mary Daly and David Dickson (Dublin: Trinity College and University College, 1990), pp. 153–166.

9. The most comprehensive and convincing attempts to ascertain the geographical patterns of Irish speaking from the eighteenth through twentieth centuries come in a series of articles by Garret Fitzgerald, who shows that on the eve of the Famine native Irish must have been far more widely spoken, in geographical terms, than had been assumed, but also that the decline in the language had been well set in motion

long before this. By analyzing the patterns of Irish speaking among the oldest age groups in the 1851 census, he is able to reconstruct—using some ingenious statistical devices—a picture of what the situation of the language must have been in individual areas almost a century before. For the clearest and most up to date summary of these results, see "The Decline of the Irish Language" in *Ireland in the World: Further Reflections* (Dublin: Liberties Press, 2005), pp. 11–22. More detailed statistics and maps, although with conclusions that Fitzgerald subsequently refined, can be found in his earlier articles: "Estimates for Baronies of Minimum Level of Irish Speaking amongst the Successive Decennial Cohorts, 1771–1781 to 1861–1871," *Proceedings of the Royal Irish Academy* 84C (1984), pp. 117–155; "The Decline of the Irish Language 1771–1871," in *The Origins of Popular Literacy in Ireland*, ed. Daly and Dickson, pp. 59–72; "Irish-Speaking in the Pre-Famine Period: A Study Based on the 1911 Census Data for People Born before 1851 and Still Alive in 1911," *Proceedings of the Royal Irish Academy* 103C (2003), pp. 191–283.

10. Popular lore attributes this change to the establishment by the British of national primary education from 1831 or to the Great Famine of 1845–1847, but as Fitzgerald ("Irish-Speaking in the Pre-Famine Period") has shown, the process of linguistic change was a more complex one that began at the opening of the nineteenth century.

11. For a history of the term and a comprehensive history of the emergence of the ideology of the Gaeltacht as a culturally distinct region, see Caitríona Ó Torna, *Cruthú na Gaeltachta 1893–1922* (Dublin: Cois Life, 2005).

12. Quoted in John Walsh, *Díchoimisiúnú Teanga: Coimisiún na Gaeltachta 1926* (Dublin: Cois Life, 2002), p. 12.

13. Quoted in Ó Torna, *Cruthú na Gaeltachta*, pp. 14–15.

14. See Reg Hindley, "Defining the Gaeltacht: Dilemmas in Irish language Planning," in *Linguistic Minorities: Society and Territory*, ed. Colin H. Williams (Clevedon: Multilingual Matters, 1991), pp. 66–95.

15. For the difficulties and unreliability of this survey, and details of some specific anomalies see Hindley, "Defining the Gaeltacht," pp. 67–71. Hindley points out that while the commission exaggerated the survival of Irish in overwhelmingly English-speaking districts adjacent to the true Gaeltacht, they overlooked genuinely Irish-speaking pockets in the midlands and east of the country. For a defense of the commission's work, see Walsh, *Díchoimisiúnú Teanga*, p. 17.

16. Ó Giolláin writes that the Gaeltacht was identified as a "reservoir of Irishness," *Locating Irish Folklore*, p. 3.

17. Quoted in Ó Torna, *Cruthú na Gaeltachta*, p. 64.

18. There was an interesting double-think in this movement which persisted through the twentieth century, of which vestiges remain today: on the one hand, it was clear that English was now too deeply rooted in everyday life to be replaced in any real way by Irish; on the other, it was important to treat the dream as though it were a reality, forming official commissions of inquiry and strategy.

19. Though in a famous formulation Yeats wrote: "Gaelic is my native tongue but it is not my mother tongue." Quoted in Michael Cronin, *Translating Ireland: Translation, Languages, Cultures* (Cork: Cork University Press, 1996), p. 142.

20. As Gréagóir Ó Dúill puts it, writing of the early 1970s, "The sociolinguistic policies of the time . . . insisted that inside every Irishman there was a frustrated fluent Gaeilgeoir trying to get out." Gréagóir Ó Dúill, "Infinite Grounds for Hope? Poetry in Irish Today," *Poetry Ireland Review*, no. 39 (Autumn 1993), p. 14.

21. For the lack of a standard and its effects on Irish language prose, see Máirtín Ó Cadhain, "Irish Prose in the Twentieth Century," in *Literature in Celtic Countries*, ed. J. E. Caerwyn Williams (Cardiff: University of Wales Press, 1971), pp. 141–142.

22. Seán Ó Tuama, *Repossessions* (Cork: Cork University Press, 1995), p. 6.

23. Quoted in Philip O'Leary, *Writing Beyond the Revival: Facing the Future in Gaelic Prose 1940–1951* (Dublin: University College Dublin Press, 2011), p. 1.

24. Ibid., pp. 153–218.

25. So much so that the Nazis set up a dedicated radio station, manned by German scholars of Irish language and folklore, which broadcast to Ireland, in Irish, for two years during the war. The Germans knew that Irish was a minority vernacular in Ireland but reasoned, perhaps inaccurately, that fluent Irish speakers were the most likely to be receptive to their anti-British broadcasts. See Clair Wills, *That Neutral Island: A Cultural History of Ireland during the Second World War* (Cambridge, MA: Harvard University Press, 2007), p. 193.

26. For an analysis of the literary characteristics and merits of the three major Blasket works, *Peig* by Peig Sayers, *Fiche Bliain ag Fás* (*Twenty Years A-Growing*) by Muiris Ó Súilleabháin, and *An tOileánach* (*The*

Islandman) by Tomás Ó Criomhthain, see Declan Kiberd, *Irish Classics* (London: Granta, 2000), pp. 520–542.

27. Ó Cadhain wrote that he found Peig Sayers's "poetic descriptions . . . of scenery difficult to swallow from a person who never left the island and its neighbourhood, and had no frame of reference for the scenery." "Irish Prose in the Twentieth Century," p. 149.

28. Gearóid Denvir, "D'Aithle na bhFilí" *Innti* 11 (Easter 1988), pp. 103–119.

29. Ibid.

30. See also Denvir, "The Living Tradition: Oral Irish Language Poetry in Connemara Today," *Éire-Ireland* 24, no. 1 (1989), pp. 92–108.

31. In contemporary Irish-language literature this group would include Nuala Ní Dhomhnaill (brought up by her relatives in Corca Dhuibhne) and Cathal Ó Searcaigh, from a native Irish-speaking community in Donegal.

32. The pattern is not, however, replicated in Breton, for example; see Favereau, "Twentieth Century Breton Literature," in *Celtic Literatures in the Twentieth Century*, ed. Séamus Mac Mathúna, Ailbhe Ó Corráin, and Maxim Fomin (Belfast: Research Institute for Irish and Celtic Studies, 2007), p. 138. Perhaps this is because, while spoken Breton has declined catastrophically, the Breton-speaking territory has never really been fragmented, the language declining chronologically, by generation, within it, and not geographically. See Humphrey Lloyd Humphreys, "The Geolinguistics of Breton," in *Linguistic Minorities, Society and Territory*, ed. Colin H. Williams (Clevedon: Multilingual Matters, 1991), pp. 96–120.

33. Quoted in Declan Kiberd, *The Irish Writer and the World* (Cambridge: Cambridge University Press, 2005), pp. 107–108.

34. Michael Cronin, "Altered States: Translation and Minority Languages," *TTR: Traduction, terminologie, rédaction* 8, no. 1 (1995), pp. 94–95, analyzes the ways Séamas Mac Annaidh—a nonnative-speaking novelist from Enniskillen who writes in Irish—plays with the language situation. On the untranslatability of Mac Annaidh's novel, *Cuaifeach mo Londubh Bhuí*, which mixes the epic of *Gilgamesh* with the surreal adventures of a man in Enniskillen, see Anthony McCann, "'Ar Lorg na Gaoithe': The Impossibility of Translating *Cuaifeach Mo Londubh Buí* into English," in *Back to the Present, Forward to the Past: Irish Writing and History Since 1798*, ed. Patricia Lynch et al. (Amsterdam: Rodopi, 2006), pp. 175–186.

35. Fiction set in an Irish-speaking world must now refer to a restricted set of highly specific locales, take place in the historical past when there

were larger Irish-speaking communities, or invent a counterfactual world. A 1929 novel in English by Michael Henry Gaffney entitled *The Boys of Ben Eadar: A School Story of 1950* (Dublin: Talbot Press, 1930), which depicts an imaginary Ireland of the future that has become wholly Irish-speaking, could plausibly have been written in Irish, for example.

36. This problem is shared by other minor languages; as Angharad Price has suggested, the fragmentation of organic Welsh-speaking communities meant that by the 1990s, the social realism that characterized the Welsh-language novel of the mid-twentieth century had become impossible to sustain without denying the linguistic realities of contemporary Wales. Quoted in Lynch, "Twentieth Century Welsh Literature," in *Celtic Literatures in the Twentieth Century*, ed. Mac Mathúna, Ó Corráin, and Fomin, p. 123. There were debates, as Alan Titley puts it, over "whether Irish could be used as a medium for urban speech, or if people who spoke English in reality could be shown to have Irish coming out of their mouths, or whether there was an appropriate subject matter for the novel in Irish." Alan Titley, "The Novel in Irish," in *The Cambridge Companion to the Irish Novel*, ed. John Wilson Foster (Cambridge: Cambridge University Press, 2006), p. 174.

37. The conundrum of who, exactly, the audience for Irish-language literature was, in a country where the active reading public almost all spoke English far better than Irish, reached its most extreme disconnect in the translation project of the government agency An Gúm, which from the 1920s through the 1940s commissioned hundreds of translations of English literary classics into Irish (at the explicit expense of commissioning original work in Irish), with print runs vastly in excess of any possible market. It appears that An Gúm did not even attempt to survey the possible extent of markets at all. See Gearóidín Uí Laighléis, "An Gúm: The Early Years," in *Celtic Literatures in the Twentieth Century*, ed. Mac Mathúna, Ó Corráin, and Fomin, p. 211.

38. In fact the inner Gaeltacht cores in south-central Connemara, western Corca Dhuibhne, and northwest Donegal remained remarkably stable until the 1970s. See Ó Riagáin, "Irish Language Production and Reproduction 1981–1996," in *Can Threatened Languages Be Saved? Reversing Language Shift, Revisited: A 21st Century Perspective*, ed. Joshua A. Fishman (Clevedon: Multilingual Matters: Clevedon, 2000), p. 203.

39. Both quoted in *An Duine is dual: Aistí ar Sheán Ó Riordáin*, ed. Eoghan Ó hAnluain (Dublin: An Clóchomhar, 1980) p. 98.

Chapter 2. The Queer Linguistic Utopia of Pier Paolo Pasolini

1. Alfredo Stussi writes: "In Italy . . . the exclusive tool of communication was, for the vast majority, dialect, and this remained substantially the case until after the Second World War [in Italia . . . lo strumento esclusivo della communicazione era, per la stragrande maggioranza, il dialetto e tale sarebbe rimasto, in sostanza, fino al secondo dopoguerra]." Stussi, "Lingua e dialetto nella tradizione letteraria italiana: Teoria e storia," in *Atti del convegno (Salerno, 5–6 novembre 1993)* (Rome: Salerno Editrice, 1996), p. 10.

2. Stussi, *Lingua, dialetto e letteratura* (Turin: Einaudi, 1993), p. 49. Stussi points out that the result of this change was not a uniformly Florentine-speaking Italy but a variety of regional forms of Italian. There is some parallel with Ireland here, in which Irish dialects were replaced by regional varieties of Hiberno-English, which reproduced the particularities of the local Gaelic.

3. For an account of the two different philological theories about Raeto-Romance, see Georg A. Kaiser, Werner Carigiet, and Mike Evans, "Raeto-Romance," in *Minor Languages of Europe: A Series of Lectures at the University of Bremen, April–July 2000*, ed. Thomas Stolz (Bochum: Universitätsverlag Dr. Norbert Brockmeyer), pp. 183–188.

4. Nicholas Ostler points out in this regard that there is evidence of a collapse of literacy in the former western empire from around 400, and that in the sixth century it could not be assumed that even merchants and businessmen could read. *Empires of the Word* (New York: Harper Collins, 2005), p. 308.

5. See Peter Burke, *Languages and Communities in Early Modern Europe* (Cambridge: Cambridge University Press, 2004), pp. 35–38.

6. As John P. Welle succinctly puts it: "From this point onward, writing in one of the numerous Italian dialects became a conscious choice: a gesture that also implied a certain polemical distance from Italian." John P. Welle, Introduction to Andrea Zanzotto, *Peasants Wake for Fellini's Casanova and Other Poems*, edited and translated by John P. Welle and Ruth Feldman (Urbana: University of Illinois Press, 1997), p. xi.

7. This oft-cited figure is from Tullio De Mauro, *Storia linguistica dell'Italia unita* (Bari: Laterza, 1984), p. 43.

8. Both examples quoted in W. Theodor Elwert, *Aufsätze zur Italienischen Lyrik* (Wiesbaden: Franz Steiner, 1967), p. 166.

9. Stussi, *Lingua, dialetto e letteratura*, p. 47.

10. Stussi writes:

> The fact that the development of the study of dialectology oc-
> curred in the decades immediately following the unification of
> Italy certainly depended on a general trend in Romance linguis-
> tics in Europe, but it was also affected by an anxious concern
> with collecting what seemed put at risk by the ongoing spread
> of Italian.
>
> [Il fatto che lo sviluppo degli studi dialettologici cada nei de-
> cenni immediatamente successivi all'Unità dipende senz'altro
> da un generale indirizzo degli studi di linguistica romanza in
> Europa, ma risente anche della sollecita preoccupazione di rac-
> cogliere quanto pare messo in pericolo dalla progressiva espan-
> sione dell'italiano.] (*Lingua, dialetto e letteratura*, p. 45)

11. De Mauro, *Storia linguistica dell'Italia unita*, pp. 126–141.

12. Ibid., pp. 149–159.

13. Franco Brevini, "Introduzione," *Poeti dialettali del Novecento* (Turin: Einaudi, 1987), p. vi.

14. Alberto A. Sobrero, "Dialetti 'coperti' e riscoperti," *Italiano e oltre* 5 (1986), p. 195.

15. Brevini, *La poesia in dialetto: Storia e testi dalle origini al Novecento*, 3 vols. (Milan: Mondadori, 1999), pp. 3205–3206.

16. Quoted ibid.

17. Resorted to by poets who, in the words of Pasolini, lived in "a civiliza-tion which has reached a crisis of language, which has reached Rim-baud's desolate and violent *'je ne sais plus parler'* [in una civiltà giunta a una sua crisi linguistica, al desolato, e violento *'je ne sais plus parler'* rimbaudiano]." Quoted in Tom O'Neill, "Pier Paolo Pasolini's Dialect Poetry," in *Forum Italicum* 9, no. 4 (December 1975), p. 343.

18. For an account of this tendency in modernist lyric, see Guido Mazzoni, *Sulla poesia moderna* (Bologna: Mulino, 2005), especially pp. 193–210.

19. Brevini, *La poesia in dialetto*, p. 3166.

20. Notably by Pullè, whose 1891 essay on Modenese dialect literature con-tained, according to Stussi, all of the essentials of Croce's ideas, and who questioned the idea that "artificial" literature in dialect came later than "natural" or "spontaneous" production. For this and for discussion of Croce's other predecessors, see Stussi, "Lingua e dialetto nella tradiz-ione letteraria italiana," pp. 13–14.

21. De Mauro, "Pasolini linguista," *Italianist* 5, no. 1 (1985), p. 67.

22. Quoted in Hideyuki Doi, *L'esperienza friulana di Pasolini: Cinque studi* (Florence: Franco Cesati Editore, 2011), p. 42.

23. Indeed, Brevini points out that the word *rosada* had in fact been used in writing by the Friulian poet Vittorio Cadèl (1884–1917), and even by the "hated" Zorutti, the eighteenth-century founder of Friulian literature. Brevini (ed.), *Dialetti e poesia del Novecento* (Milan: Mondadori, 1999), vol. 3, p. 3197, note 42.

24. Doi, *L'esperienza friulana di Pasolini*, pp. 175–176.

25. De Mauro, "Pasolini linguista," p. 67.

26. Linda Picco, in *Ricercje su la condizion sociolenghistiche dal furlan* (Udine: Editrice Universitaria Udinese, 2001), pp. 31–32, reports that in Friuli 75 percent of the generation born at the beginning of the twentieth century spoke Friulian, a rate that had halved by the 1970s. She estimates that in the second half of the twentieth century—the decades immediately following Pasolini's Friulian phase—the average loss in the language is at a rate of 10 percent per generation.

27. Brevini writes: "Until Pasolini, every poet went along his own path, in a dialectical relationship with his own regional tradition. Awareness of what was being done in dialect beyond one's own village was limited to Neapolitan. [Fino a Pasolini ogni poeta faceva la sua strada, in un rapporto dialettico con la propria tradizione regionale. La conoscenza di ciò che in dialetto si faceva al di fuori del proprio campanile si limitava al napoletano.]" Brevini, *La poesia in dialetto*, pp. 3200–3201.

28. Quoted by O'Neill, "Pier Paolo Pasolini's Dialect Poetry," p. 356.

29. References for Pasolini's poetry are to *Pasolini: Tutte le poesie*, ed. Walter Siti, 2 vols. (Milan: Mondadori, 2003).

30. "His passion for the Friulian dialect, in itself a muted form of anti-Fascism, contributed to the development of a poetics that located him at the centre of debates in Italian culture but was inseparable from his erotic attachment to the peasant boys of Friuli." Derek Duncan, *Reading and Writing Italian Homosexuality: A Case of Possible Difference* (London: Ashgate, 2005), p. 92.

31. Brevini suggests that the homosexual component of his vision had wider European connections: "But the exquisite puppet theater that [Pasolini] constructs, inhabited by ephebes in rustic peasant dress, redrawn in a nervous modernist line, is nothing other than the dramatization of an anxious Gidean psychology [Ma lo squisito teatrino che

[Pasolini] costruisce, popolato di efebi in rustiche vesti contandine, ridisegnati da un nervoso segno liberty, non è che la drammatizzazione di un'inquieta psicologia gidiana]." Brevini, *Dialetti e poesia del Novecento*, p. 3196.

32. Ulick O'Connor, *Brendan Behan* (London: Hamilton, 1970), pp. 71–79. For a more comprehensive account of Behan's relationship with Ó Briain (who was among those who denied Behan's homosexuality) see Michael O'Sullivan, *Brendan Behan: A Life* (Dublin: Blackwater, 1999), passim.

33. O'Connor, *Brendan Behan*, p. 79.

34. Ibid., p. 126.

35. Ibid., p. 115.

36. "Oscar Wilde Poète et Dramaturge, né à Dublin le 15 Octobre, 1856, est mort dans cette maison le 30 Novembre, 1900," in which Behan envies his dead idol, because "you had it every way [bhí sé agat gach bealach]."

37. An Crann faoi Bhláth / The Flowering Tree: Contemporary Irish Poetry, ed. Declan Kiberd and Gabriel Fitzmaurice (Dublin: Wolfhound, 1991), p. 108.

38. Piera Rizzolati, "Il percorso friulano di Pier Paolo Pasolini," in *Pasolini tra friulano e romanesco*, ed. Marcello Teodonio (Rome: Colombo, 1997), p. 11.

39. For a narratological account of this structural predicament of homosexuality, see Barry McCrea, *In the Company of Strangers: Family and Narrative in Dickens, Conan Doyle, Joyce, and Proust* (New York: Columbia University Press, 2011), especially pp. 8–14.

40. Doi, *L'esperienza friulana di Pasolini*, p. 169.

41. Seán Ó Ríordáin, "Teangacha príobháideacha," *Scríobh* 4 (1979), pp. 12–22.

42. See *Pasolini tra friulano e romanesco*, ed. Teodonio, passim.

43. Quoted in Doi, *L'esperienza friulana di Pasolini*, p. 42.

44. Pasolini favorably revised his view of Italian in later decades, when the standard language was no longer restricted to an elite social class. He thought, in 1964, that a new linguistic reality was being born in Italy: "Italian," he wrote, "has been born as a national language [è nato l'italiano come lingua nazionale]," quoted in De Mauro, "Pasolini linguista," p. 69.

45. Though Zanzotto was already reflecting in his poetry in *lingua* on the disappearance of dialect as a theme: "Pace per me, per voi / buona gente

senza più dialetto" (in Welle's translation: "Peace to me, to you / good people who no longer possess a dialect"). Quoted in Welle, Introduction to Zanzotto, *Peasants Wake*, p. ix.

46. Quoted in Doi, *L'esperienza friulana di Pasolini*, p. 41.

Chapter 3. Seán Ó Ríordáin's Private Language

1. Diarmaid Ó Doibhlin writes: "There can be little doubt in my view that Seán Ó Ríordáin, despite a relatively small output, is the most significant Irish language poet of the twentieth century." "Twentieth Century Irish Poetry: *Dath Géime na mBó*," in *Celtic Literatures in the Twentieth Century*, ed. Séamus Mac Mathúna, Ailbhe Ó Corráin, and Maxim Fomin (Belfast: Research Institute for Irish and Celtic Studies, 2007), p. 32. For the most comprehensive and detailed analysis (in Irish) of Ó Ríordáin's contribution, his influences, and the nature of his poetics see Seán Ó Tuama, "Seán Ó Ríordáin agus an Nuafhilíocht," *Studia Hibernica* 13 (1973), pp. 100–167.

2. Quoted in Hideyuki Doi, *L'esperienza friulana di Pasolini: Cinque studi* (Florence: Franco Cesati Editore, 2011), p. 41.

3. Ó Tuama, for example, writes: "Seán Ó Ríordáin spent *fifteen years* of his youth in Ballyvourney, when Irish was still the ordinary spoken language of the adult generation there; he spoke Irish naturally from the start; he spoke Irish constantly and usually with his grandmother who was next door to him; if he was not a native speaker of Irish, he was not a native speaker of English either [Chaith Seán Ó Ríordáin *cúig bliana déag* dá óige i mBaile Mhúirne, nuair b'í an Ghaeilge fós gnáth-theanga labhartha na ndaoine fásta ann; gur labhair sé an Ghaeilge go nádúrtha ó thosach; gur labhair sé an Ghaeilge de shíor is de ghnáth lena sheanamhátháir a bhí i mbéal an dorais aige; munar cainteoir dúchais Gaeilge é nach cainteoir dúchais Béarla é ach an oiread]" (emphasis in original). Quoted in Máirín Nic Eoin, *Trén bhFearann Breac: An Díláithriú Cultúir agus Nualitríocht na Gaeilge* (Dublin: Cois Life, 2005), p. 70.

4. Ó Ríordáin, "An Ghaeltacht agus fairsingiú na teangan," *Comhar* 13, no. 12 (December 1954), p. 10.

5. When Ó Ríordáin applied for his post in the Motor Taxation Office, in the section of the application form asked to provide evidence of knowledge of the Irish language, he entered the ambiguous phrase "Tógadh mé sa Ghaeltacht," "I was brought up in the Gaeltacht."

6. Quoted in Seán Ó Coileáin, *Seán Ó Ríordáin: Beatha agus Saothar* (Dublin: An Clóchomhar, 1985), p. 242.

7. Quoted in ibid., pp. 314–315.

8. In "Banfhilíocht agus Gaeilge," *Irish Times*, November 27, 1975, Ó Ríordáin recalls that he: "listened to the best Irish from when I came out of the oven. . . . My grandmother and aunt lived next door to me and they spoke Irish among themselves [ag éisteacht le togha na Gaeilge ó thánag as an oigheann. . . . Bhí mo sheanmhathair agus aintín dom ag béal an dorais laistior díom agus is as Gaeilge a labhraidís eatarthu féin]."

9. Ó Tuama, "Seán Ó Ríordáin agus an Nuafhilíocht," p. 101, writes: "Irish was about to fade in Baile Bhuirne at that time. It was mostly English that was spoken in his own home, since his mother did not know much Irish. The younger generation most often spoke English among themselves. However, Irish was by far the richer and more proficient language in the mouths of the people of the area. It was the literary language of the place. It was the language of the old people and of the middle-aged. It was often the language of the home. It was the ordinary language of the family in his grandmother's house, one of the neighboring houses that Ó Ríordáin most often frequented when he was a child. [Bhí an Ghaeilge ar tí leá i mBaile Bhuirne an tráth sin. Béarla is mó a bhíodh á labhairt ar a theallach féin, mar nach raibh mórán Gaeilge ag a mháthair. Béarla is minicí a labhraíodh an t-aos óg eatarthu féin ach amháin i gclós na scoile. Ba í an Ghaeilge, áfach, an teanga ba shaibhre is ba chumasaí go mór fada ar bhéala daoine sa dúthaigh. Ba í teanga liteartha na háite í. Ba í teanga na seandaoine is na ndaoine meánaosta í. Ba í teanga an teallaigh go minic í. Ba í gnáth-theanga na muintire í i dteach a sheanmháthar, ceann de na tithe comharsan is mó a ghnáthaíodh an Ríordánach is é ina leanbh.]"

10. Ó Tuama points out that while Irish was ceasing to be the vehicle of everyday communication in the Baile Bhuirne of Ó Ríordáin's childhood, it had remained the literary language of the community, and "a large amount of verse mostly based on eighteenth and nineteenth-century models, was still being composed in the district." *Repossessions* (Cork: Cork University Press, 1995), p. 11.

11. See the interviews with them in the documentary by Traolach Ó Buachalla and Louis de Paor, *Mise Seán Ó Ríordáin* (TG4, 2007).

12. Ibid.

13. Quoted in Ó Coileáin, *Seán Ó Ríordáin*, p. 78.

14. Ó Ríordáin's correspondence in Irish with Séamus Ó Coigligh, however, is frank, emotional, and openly affectionate.

15. Quoted in Ó Coileáin, *Seán Ó Ríordáin*, p. 307.

16. For an account of how this linguistic division might have affected Ó Ríordáin's poetry, see Ó Tuama, "Seán Ó Ríordáin agus an Nuafhilíocht," p. 163.

17. John A. Murphy writes that, for Ó Ríordáin, "there was nothing of value in modern Ireland apart from the remnants of Gaelic culture. There could be nothing of worth in the country in the future if it did not return to Gaelicness . . . he had little time for Ireland outside the Gaeltacht (or perhaps outside Dún Chaoin!). Ireland outside the Gaeltacht was a desert. . . . Only in the Gaeltacht, according to Seán, could one find heritage, reality, conversation, personalities, characters. 'Compared to Dún Chaoin,' he said, 'towns like Macroom and Cobh [English-speaking towns in Co. Cork] are as good as dead' [ní raibh de fhiúntas in Éirinn an lae inniu ach ach an t-iarsma Gaelach. Ní bheadh puinn maitheasa sa tír seo sa todhchaí mura bhfillfeadh sí ar an nGaelachas. . . . Ba bheag leis Éire lasmuigh den Ghaeltacht (nó b'fhéidir lasmuigh de Dhún Chaoin!). Fásach ab ea Éire lasmuigh den Ghaeltacht. . . . Sa Ghaeltacht amháin, dar le Seán, a bhí an dúchas, an réadúlacht, comhrá, cultúr, pearsana, carachtair. 'I gcomórtas le Dún Chaoin,' dúirt sé, 'tá bailte ar nós Má Chromtha agus Cóbh geall le bheith marbh']." (Ó Ríordáin took particular delight in saying this, according to Murphy, since he knew that Murphy himself had grown up in Macroom). *An Duine is dual: Aistí ar Sheán Ó Riordáin*, ed. Eoghan Ó hAnluain (Dublin: An Clóchomhar, 1980), p. 136.

18. Declan Kiberd has persuasively suggested Ó Ríordáin wrote in "an Irish as English as it is reasonably possible for that language to be," and that one might view the case of Ó Ríordáin as a "kind of inversion of the case of Synge [cineál inbheartú ar chás Synge]." Kiberd, in *An Duine is dual*, ed. Ó hAnluain, p. 93. "In the case of Ó Ríordáin," he writes, "ideas were coming to him thick and fast in English, modern ideas that often had nothing to do with the old Gaelic mindset or the old beliefs of Dún Chaoin [i gcás an Ríordánaigh bhí smaointe ag teacht chuige go tiubh as Béarla, smaointe nua-aimseartha go minic nár bhain puinn leis an seanaigne Ghaelach ná le seanchreideamh Dhún Chaoin]." *An Duine is dual*, ed. Ó hAnluain, p. 101.

19. Ó Tuama, *Repossessions*, p. 12.

20. This is a very literal translation of my own; an excellent poetic translation by Paul Muldoon can be found in *Seán Ó Ríordáin: Selected Poems*, ed. Frank Sewell (New Haven: Yale University Press, 2014), pp. 46–51.

21. Ó Tuama, *Repossessions*, p. 12.
22. Ó Tuama, "Seán Ó Ríordáin agus an Nuafhilíocht," p. 106.
23. Ibid.
24. Ó Tuama, "Seán Ó Ríordáin," in *The Pleasures of Gaelic Poetry*, ed. Seán Mac Réamoinn (London: Viking, 1982), p. 129.
25. Ibid.
26. For a fuller account of this aspect of the poem, see Barry McCrea, "Adhlacadh an Bhéarla," *Comhar* (August 2012), p. 23.
27. Ó Coileáin, *Seán Ó Ríordáin*, p. 95, quotes the letter in full.
28. For a probing analysis of these lines and of the poem as a whole, see Louis de Paor, "Adhlacadh mo Mháthar," in *Irish University Review: A Journal of Irish Studies*, Special Irish Poetry Issue, guest ed. Peter Denman (September 2009).
29. Gilles Deleuze and Félix Guattari, "Minor Literature: Kafka," in *The Deleuze Reader*, ed. Constantin Boundas (New York: Columbia University Press, 1993), p. 152.
30. Quoted in Ó Coileáin, *Seán Ó Ríordáin*, pp. 246–247.
31. Ibid. p. 249.
32. Ibid. p. 248.
33. Quoted in Ó Ríordáin, "Comhfhreagras agus Conspóid," *Comhar* 46, no. 2 (February 1987), pp. 31–33.
34. Review by Flann Mac an tSaoir, *Comhar* 10, no. 12 (December 1951), p. 7.
35. We might thus identify three levels of surviving native Irish in the first half of the twentieth century: the Irish of places like Tumgesh, tainted with the horrors of the Famine and condemned to traumatized silence (the Limerick Irish that Michael Hartnett picked up from his grandmother might be considered another example of this); the Irish of Baile Bhuirne, fading out of vernacular use but still widely known and respected; and finally, the Irish of Dún Chaoin, Gaoth Dobhair or Connemara, a medium of everyday life and culture.
36. "Ó Ríordáin is right to remind us that there is hardly any form of contemporary thought that cannot be expressed in Irish. The risk for him is that he might think that he has expressed an idea when in fact it is not Irish he has written at all [Tá an ceart ag an Ríordánach a chur i gcuimhne dúinn nach móide go bhfuil aon ghné d'intinn an lae inniu nach féidir a chur in iúl sa Ghaeilge. Sé an baol dó ná a cheapadh go bhfuil smaoineamh léirithe aige nuair nach Gaeilge in aon chor an rud atá scríofa aige]." Quoted in Ó Coileáin, *Seán Ó Ríordáin*, p. 239.

37. Mhac an tSaoi, "Scríbhneoireacht sa Ghaeilge Inniu," *Studies: An Irish Quarterly Review* 44, no. 173 (Spring 1955), p. 88.

38. Máire Mhac an tSaoi, "Filíocht Sheáin Uí Ríordáin," *Feasta* (March 1953), pp. 17–19 (p. 17), and "Scríbhneoireacht sa Ghaeilge Inniu," pp. 88–89. The translations here are by de Paor, which I have slightly modified.

39. Quoted in Ó Coileáin, *Seán Ó Ríordáin*, p. 240.

40. See ibid., pp. 234–266.

41. Caoimhín Mac Giolla Léith, "Contemporary Poetry in Irish: Private Languages and Ancestral Voices," in *Poetry in Contemporary Irish Literature*, ed. Michael Kenneally (Lanham, MD: Rowman and Littlefield, 1995), p. 88.

42. Matty Byrne, who died in 1942 at the age of eighty-four, was the last native speaker of Kilkenny Irish. See *The Language of Kilkenny: Lexicon, Semantics, Structures*, ed. Séamas Moylan (Dublin: Geography Publications, 1996), p. 383. Dates for the last native speakers from other counties vary somewhat, partly because of ambiguity surrounding the term "native speaker" (especially the question of whether or not people who learned the language from their native-speaking grandparents but who spoke English as their own first language—useful informants for philologists like Wagner—should qualify). Some of the dates given for the death of the last native speakers, hard to verify, are as follows: Tyrone 1952, Antrim 1974, Armagh 1952, Louth 1962, Sligo 1980—although this last date, for example, was to be proven inaccurate by the Deasy brothers of Culdaly, Kilmacthigue who lived until 1999.

43. Quoted in Ó Coileáin, *Seán Ó Ríordáin*, p. 370.

44. Ó Cadhain, who admired Ó Ríordáin, seems to have had an ambiguous position on this. On the one hand, he worries that "learners—who constitute most of the writers today—have sinned against the language, both through ignorance and by trying to make words do things which words in a particular language may not be capable of." On the other, he says, in the same breath, without apparent regret, that "if Irish is revived as the language of any considerable setion of our people it will change out of all recognition." "Irish Prose in the Twentieth Century," in *Literature in Celtic Countries*, ed. J. E. Caerwyn Williams (Cardiff: University of Wales Press, 1971), p. 144.

45. Quoted in Ó Cóileáin, *Seán Ó Ríordáin*, p. 78.

46. Ibid., p. 105.

47. Quoted in Caitríona Ó Torna, *Cruthú na Gaeltachta 1893–1922* (Dublin: Cois Life, 2005), p. 144.

48. Ó Coileáin, *Seán Ó Ríordáin*, pp. 314–315.

49. A number of Irish-language writers seem to hint that Irish is the language of the lost or absent father—Nuala Ní Dhomhnaill has said that writing in Irish was "a way to my father's heart." Interview with Laura O'Connor, *Southern Review* (Summer 1995), p. 587. One might identify something of the same psychoanalytical framework in operation in the case of Flann O'Brien, whose father, the chief source of Irish in the home, was a mostly absent figure.

50. Mac Giolla Léith, "Contemporary Poetry in Irish," p. 84.

51. Ibid.

52. Ibid.

53. Quoted in Brevini, *La poesia in dialetto: Storia e testi dalle origini al Novecento*, 3 vols. (Milan: Mondadori, 1999), p. 3166.

54. Ibid.

55. Benedetto Croce, "Note sulla letteratura italiana: Salvatore di Giacomo," *La Critica* 1, no. 6 (November 20, 1903), p. 423.

56. Michael Hartnett, A Farewell to English and Other Poems (Dublin: Gallery Books, 1975), p. 35.

57. For an account of Munster Irish as the literary dialect, see Ó Dúill, "Infinite Grounds for Hope? Poetry in Irish Today," *Poetry Ireland Review*, no. 39 (Autumn 1993), pp. 15–16.

58. According to Ó Tuama, who was less impressed with some of Ó Ríordáin's subsequent output, *Brosna* was "one of the most distinguished volumes of verse ever published in Ireland." Ó Tuama, *Repossessions*, p. 19.

59. Seamus Heaney, "Forked Tongues, Céilís and Incubators," *Fortnight* (September 1983), p. 20.

60. Ó Tuama, "Seán Ó Ríordáin," in *The Pleasures of Gaelic Poetry*, ed. Mac Réamoinn, p. 135.

61. Heaney, "Forked Tongues," p. 21.

62. In his own life, Ó Ríordáin frequently reiterated a vague intention of leaving Inniscarra for good and going to live in the Gaeltacht, something which he never managed to do, and which strikes me as being a necessary fiction that tallies with the idea that native Irish functioned principally for him as something to long for—see, for example, this revealing exchange in "Tagann na rudaí ar ais chugat" ["Things come back to you"], p. 29:

"But you are living in Cork, so are there two sides to your poetry? Is Cork, as a city, important to you?"

"No. I can't explain that, except maybe, health reasons. . . . I ought to move to the Gaeltacht. Well I ought to spend the greater part of the year in the Gaeltacht. I don't spend the greater part of the year in the Gaeltacht and . . . Cork is no help to me."

["Ach tá tú ag maireachtaint i gCorcaigh, an bhfuil an dá thaobh mar sin le do chuid scríbhneoireachta. An bhfuil Corcaigh, mar chathair, tábhachtach duit?"

"Níl. Ní féidir liom é sin a mhíniú ach amháin b'fhéidir cúrsaí sláinte. . . . ba cheart dom aistriú go dtí an Ghaeltacht. Bhuel ba cheart dom an chuid is mó den bhliain a chaitheamh sa Ghaeltacht. Ní chaithim an chuid is mó den bhliain sa Ghaeltacht agus . . . ní haon chabhair dom Corcaigh."]

63. This text is from *Séan Ó Ríordáin: Selected Poems*, ed. Sewell, pp. 162–163; translation by Barry McCrea.

64. It is called Gleann na nGealt, "Valley of the Mad," because the water from a spring in the valley is said to cure mental illness.

65. For an account of the literary refractions of the Irish myth of the West, see Luke Gibbons, "Synge, Country and Western: The Myth of the West in Irish and American Culture," in *Culture and Ideology in Ireland*, ed. Chris Curtin, Mary Kelly, and Liam O'Dowd (Galway: Galway University Press, 1984).

66. Heaney, "Forked Tongues," p. 20.

67. Tom O'Neill, while granting that the Casarsa of Pasolini's poetry is not a real place but rather a *paese dell'anima*, a landscape of the soul, writes that "Pasolini's withdrawal into the Casarsa of his youth is, in its way, a withdrawal from the unacceptable reality of fascist Italy, a rejection of history." Tom O'Neill, "Pier Paolo Pasolini's Dialect Poetry," *Forum Italicum* 9, no. 4 (December 1975), p. 345.

68. As did the so-called *Innti* generation of poets after him whom he influenced. For an account in English, both critical and appreciative, of the *Innti* writers, their place, and their influence, see Ó Dúill, "Infinite Grounds for Hope?"; for an insider's account see Michael Davitt, "Uige an Chuimhnimh" *Comhar* 43, no. 12 (December 1984), pp. 32–35; for a summary of how the *Innti* group fits into the overall development of

twentieth-century Irish-language writing, see Ó Tuama, *Repossessions*, pp. 7–9.

Chapter 4. The Great Silence in Combray

1. Indeed, Pétain's cult of the French peasant was to be intimately wrapped up with violent hatred of the "rootless" Jew.

2. There is a sympathetic account in the *Recherche* of the difficulties of a Breton-speaking soldier in the army who "learned French with as much difficulty as if it had been English or German" (III.181–182) ["Ayant appris le français aussi difficilement que s'il eût été anglais ou allemand" (III.i.131)]. I cite for English the six-volume Modern Library edition: *In Search of Lost Time*, translated by C. K. Scott Moncrieff and Terence Kilmartin, revised by D. J. Enright (New York: Modern Library, 1993), and for French the seven-volume Gallimard edition: *À la Recherche du temps perdu* (Paris: Gallimard, 1987–1989), in which vol. III is divided into III.i and III.ii. References are to volume and page number.

3. Albert Dauzat, *Les Patois* (Paris: Delagrave, 1927), p. 138. Writing in 1946, Auguste Brun reports that "it would hardly be an exaggeration to say that in the environs of Paris—from the Eure to the Meuse, and from the Oise to the Berry—dialect has practically disappeared [on exagérerait à peine en disant qu'autour de Paris,—de l'Eure à la Meuse, et de l'Oise au Berry,—les dialectes ont pratiquement disparu]." Brun, *Parlers régionaux: France dialectale et unité française* (Paris: Didier, 1946), pp. 126–127.

4. See Introduction; quoted in Seán de Fréine, *The Great Silence* (Cork: Mercier Press, 1978), p. 74.

5. Chip Long, "Dialogism or Domination? Language use in Proust's *À la recherche du temps perdu*," *MLN* 111, no. 4 (September 1996), p. 768.

6. Brun, *Parlers régionaux*, p. 111.

7. I am grateful to Kevin Whelan for helping me with this formulation.

8. I owe this insight to Éric Trudel.

9. Brun, *Parlers régionaux*, p. 129.

INDEX